Praise for *Hope Leans Forward: Braving Your Way toward Simplicity, Awakening, and Peace*

"This extraordinary book is like a great river that delivers nutrients to all those on her shores. I have sat with the wisdom that Valerie Brown has shared in this remarkable volume and been uplifted and also grounded as she opens the heart of her reader through the courage and hope that she shares."

—**Roshi Joan Halifax, abbot, Upaya Zen Center**

"While reading *Hope Leans Forward*, I found myself taking deeper breaths and feeling more relaxed in my body. Valerie Brown is a skilled teacher and storyteller. She demonstrates through her experience and vulnerability, and through the wisdom of those with whom she has journeyed, how to cultivate (as Quakers say) 'the seed of God within' during a deeply challenging time. To read this book is to feel more grounded and alive; to practice the wisdom within it is to open yourself to the possibilities of your own life."

—**Barry Crossno, general secretary, Friends General Conference**

"In this moment, when our interconnectedness and mutual vulnerability are more evident than ever, Valerie Brown's *Hope Leans Forward* offers a path luminescent in its pragmatism, crystal in its invitation to shared responsibility, gentle in its guiding steps and full of grace for each of us. You will want to keep this book near and refer to it again and again."

—Sarah Willie-LeBreton, provost and dean of the faculty, professor of sociology and Black studies, Swarthmore College

"Each chapter of *Hope Leans Forward* by Valerie Brown is an exploration of one of seven factors of awakening of Buddhist teaching and practice—mindfulness, investigation, energy, joy, tranquility, concentration, and equanimity—in dialogue with Quaker tradition. In particular, Brown writes as a Buddhist-Quaker grounded in her practice of Kundalini Yoga. The end result is an excellent example of how the practice of interreligious dialogue more often than not expands one's faith journey in unexpected and creative ways."

—Paul Ingram, The Society for Buddhist-Christian Studies

"This wonderful book invites you in with its mix of warmth and empathy skillfully blended with a sense of adventure, discovery, and fun. It is rich, yet meant to be carried lightly. Practical, but in the service of the journey toward unknowing. Filled with helpful practices and powerful insights, it will help anyone chart the course toward spiritual maturity."

—Rev. Seifu Anil Singh-Molares, executive director, Spiritual Directors International

"Valerie Brown beautifully demonstrates that each of us truly has our own unique path to set and way of navigating the world. She shares her own courageous and emotional spiritual journey and the captivating and perspective-widening stories of those she met along the way. *Hope Leans Forward* is equal parts inspirational and practical offering an abundance of wisdom and guidance at the intersection of multiple religious and spiritual traditions."

—**Lynn Screen, managing director, Institute for Transformational Leadership, Georgetown University School of Continuing Studies**

"In *Hope Leans Forward* Valerie Brown intimately weaves her own story and those of others to explore in a very deep way the seven factors of awakening in Buddhism and the inquiry and reflection of Quaker spirituality to provide a reader's guide-book to explore life's deepest questions, navigate life's inevitable rocky waters and hurt places, and cultivate clarity on the way to their true self. This is a book to be read slowly, digested, and read again as it invites readers into deep reflection and uncovers the wisdom of the soul."

—**Bill Pullen, MSOD, MCC, academic director, Institute for Transformational Leadership, Georgetown University School of Continuing Studies**

"My beloved sister in the Dharma, Valerie Brown offers all of us a beautiful stream of living inspiration and wisdom born of experience. Enjoy these precious and practical life stories. If you wish to be uplifted, this is a worthy read."

—Dr. Larry Ward, The Lotus Institute and Buddhist Dharma teacher, Plum Village

"Valerie Brown's story of her journey helps me to see my own path in greater clarity. I am inspired by her courage, her boldness, her clarity. I will be using this book in my classroom and in my practice with clients. This is an inspired offering by a wonderful soul friend, and I am grateful."

—Dr. Peggy Rowe-Ward, coauthor of *Making Friends with Time* and *Love's Garden,* The Lotus Institute and Buddhist Dharma teacher, Plum Village

"If you are ready to lean into 'the discomfort that foreshadows transformation,' then this book is for you. If you are not ready for that discomfort, this book is for you. If you don't know whether you're ready for the foreshadowing, this book is for you. If you think you leaned too far into transformation, this book is for you. If you think you need to lean backwards, this book is for you. If you are not sure about your body's posture toward courage, this book is for you. In each case, Valerie Brown shows us how transformation, with just a slight pivot, is within our reach."

—Pamela Ayo Yetunde, ThD, coeditor of *Black and Buddhist: What Buddhism Can Teach Us about Race, Resilience, Transformation, and Freedom*

"Valerie Brown invites readers on a pilgrimage to the intersections of vulnerability, community, and courage—to our own soul stories. Journeying with us across challenging terrain as companion and guide, she brings the voices of other travelers she's met on her path, as well as trustworthy practices that will support and encourage us along the way—ones we can turn to whenever we need to come home to ourselves."

—**Kathryn A. McElveen, executive director,**
Center for Courage & Renewal

"As manager of QuakerBooks of the Friends General Conference, I am regularly asked about books on settling in, focusing, centering, etc. Many Friends and seekers know 'why' and they need to know 'how.' *Hope Leans Forward* will be my answer. Valerie Brown invites the reader: 'Sail with me. Let this book guide you.' She certainly delivers. Her meshing of Buddhist practices with the Quaker Way, in clear and concise words, is a gift that will guide many to mindfulness."

—**Audrey L. Greenhall, manager, QuakerBooks and**
QuakerPress, Friends General Conference

"Reading what Valerie Brown has written is a pilgrimage in itself—in the company of a wise, compassionate guide. The beautiful weaving of story and practice, the dance between Buddhist and Quaker practices, the simplicity of it, the elegance of it, the stories of Valerie's life, the stories of others who have been on this path—all these rich elements woven together in a tapestry create an experience of life's pilgrimage. I read it very slowly, allowing it to nourish me. I didn't want it to end."

—**Judy Sorum Brown, poet, writer,**
and leadership development expert

"I am beyond grateful for Valerie Brown's book *Hope Leans Forward*. Read and take in her wisdom. Begin to create your path toward bravery. We will all be better for it."

—**Yvonne L. Moore, philanthropic advisor,**
catalyst, and change agent

"Valerie Brown has written a heartful and generous book that weaves together her spiritual journey as a Catholic-Quaker-Buddhist Black woman of Cuban-Jamaican descent into a tapestry that leaves nothing behind, that honors every step of the journey—joyful and challenging alike, and that centers the voices of ordinary, extraordinary people living lives of courage and compassion in communities across the country."

—**Elaine Retholtz, licensed acupuncturist and teacher,**
New York Insight Meditation Center

hope leans forward

HOPE LEANS FORWARD

BRAVING YOUR WAY TOWARD SIMPLICITY, AWAKENING, AND PEACE

BY VALERIE BROWN

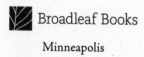

Broadleaf Books

Minneapolis

HOPE LEANS FORWARD
Braving Your Way toward Simplicity, Awakening, and Peace

Poem used with permission by Gregory Orr.
The Noble Eightfold Path used with permission by Lion's Roar Magazine.
Circle of Trust Touchstones used with permission by Center for Courage
& Renewal.
Queries from Bethesda Friends Meeting used with permission by Bethesda
Friends.

Cover design: Studio Gearbox

Print ISBN: 978-1-5064-7837-1
eBook ISBN: 978-1-5064-7838-8

Printed in Canada

While I was finishing this book, on January 22, 2022, our beloved teacher, Zen master Thich Nhat Hanh, transitioned his body. His life was celebrated for many days by millions of people around the globe. I dedicate this book to him, to his life and legacy that profoundly transformed my life and the lives of countless people.

This book is dedicated to my beloved brothers, Trevor Holtham, who passed away on February 20, 2020, and Milton Brown, who passed away on April 26, 2022. My life has changed forever because you were there for me.

CONTENTS

CONTENTS

CONTENTS

CONTENTS

INTRODUCTION

"Complications are auspicious; do not resist them."
—*"The Song of the Jewel Mirror Samādhi"*

Many people reach out to me in the passages of their lives. Sometimes it's because they've lost a thread of meaning or misplaced the small messages of hope that once led them to the center of their lives. They are treading deep waters of discontent without navigational aids. They dwell in uncertainty yet hope for clear seeing. They admire courage yet live in fear. They are seduced by control but secretly want to surrender. They crave a generous heart yet constrict it with deadly self-criticism, cynicism, and self-doubt.

I am constantly astonished and humbled by the people who find their way to me, seeking guidance because of the many roles I hold and the varying work I do in the world. As a Buddhist Dharma teacher (*Dharmacharya*), Quaker, facilitator, spiritual director,[1] retreat and pilgrimage leader, writer, and leadership coach (all after a twenty-year career as a lawyer-lobbyist), I am often contacted by potential spiritual directees, mentees, coachees, and pilgrims, as well as religious organizations, universities, and nonprofits. Sometimes a person who listened to one of my many Dharma talks or was moved by something I wrote reaches out to me because something vital and vibrant isn't working in their life.

In the people who find their way to me, the glow of their guiding inner compass, their True Self, their soul, has dimmed to a faint light. Seized by a persistent, cannot-ignore-it longing, these seekers of diverse identities, ages, races, sexual orientations, genders, socioeconomic backgrounds, and faith traditions seek me out, often with great urgency. Much like the wayfarers of ancient times, these individuals and organizations can no longer rely on tools of the past that have brought them to an unfulfilled, unresolved, or ambiguous point where there are questions without easy answers. The navigational devices—the map, guide, compass, or sextant—can't get them where they want to go. They are being called to a living observation of the stars, the sun, the ocean swells, and other signs that point the way to a new location and direction. They are moving toward the soul, the True Self, and their deepest longing.

Maybe, like them, you also are holding these feelings and that is what drew you to this book. Wherever you are on your spiritual awakening, your life's journey, I trust you'll find resources here to guide you toward what is most meaningful. In this book, I offer observations about guiding principles and patterns that I've seen emerge over time—first in my own life and then with others.

Out of necessity, I have been wayfinding through my own life, noticing the smallest signals that were calling me into a journey toward a more robust and authentic version of myself. Even now, in a mature time of my life, I am drawn to create a vision of myself larger and more expansive than I could imagine or understand, even as hope seemed ungraspable and distant for such a long time. Like many people, maybe like you, I've had it rough during the last few years with the global pandemic and the full-on reality of climate change. I've half-jokingly said that over the last several years, since 2016, I've been in my own global pandemic and the rest of the world has joined me.

Perhaps you know the feeling of being pulled—at times uncontrollably by a myriad of converging, almost inconceivable life circumstances—into full-blown crisis. Mine began when my father died in 2016. Our relationship was complicated. He did what he could, and that was pretty bad. But despite his walking out on us as kids, despite his raging out of control, his workaholism, after years of keeping him at a safe distance, after years of hoping he'd be different or the relationship would be different, I accepted him, and he accepted me. I accepted who he was and what he did and that I deserved better but didn't get that from an imperfect, very human person. We reconciled.

I made my peace, selfishly because I knew if I didn't transform the rage I had learned from him, I would pass it on to others, and it would consume me. I flew back from the United Kingdom, where I was leading retreats, to be by his bedside when he took his last breath. He looked at me and took my hand. I was there for him, and he knew it. The rage had become something else, something softer, something that felt more like forgiveness.

The complications continued when my mostly distant and painfully ambiguous marriage of 15 years fell apart in 2018 and my then-partner moved out in 2019. I remarried late in life and was totally unprepared to truly love, having inherited so much of my dad's seething rage. In the marriage, there was a kind of false hope and wishful thinking (delusion really) that maybe, despite all the warning signs, things would work out. It did for a while, until it didn't.

About the same time, my beloved brother Trevor was slowly dying of chronic heart failure. Day by day, his heart was getting fainter, weaker, until he needed around-the-clock skilled care and went into a crappy nursing home on the Upper West Side of Manhattan, the same place his wife of more than thirty years was living due to her advanced Parkinson's disease. (Little did I know that heart disease was prevalent in my family. In 2017, my brother Lewis received a heart transplant after more than a month in ICU.) Despite it all, I kept hoping that somehow Trevor would beat the odds, that he'd regain health. But he didn't. He died in February 2020, and then his wife, Gwyn, died six months later, and I hit a thick fog of grief. I ate but couldn't taste anything. Spring and then summer arrived, but I hardly noticed the flowering trees. Where was hope now?

Then in March 2020, the global pandemic of COVID-19 brought quarantine, lockdown, and death to millions of people worldwide. Context matters. I am writing specifically from my perspective as a Black woman of Cuban-Jamaican descent living on the East Coast of the United States through a global pandemic. Like many other people who carry a social group identity that is marginalized because of race and gender, I can relate to the disproportionate impact the global pandemic has had on Black and brown people and other marginalized groups. I recognize too that the world is changing fast. The realities of the global climate crisis are real, and its effects on developing nations are disproportionately felt. My life, and perhaps yours too, has been touched by the consequences of global warming. Strangely, when did we become accustomed to floods, excessive heat waves, uncontrolled fires, and drought? Perhaps for the first time, we are gravely aware that we share this planet, that we are interconnected despite our differing locations in the world and differing beliefs and values. What happens in Wuhan, China affects people in San Francisco, United States.

As happened to many people, the initial months of COVID-19 brought an abrupt end to a large part of my income. Family and friends got sick or died. As the global pandemic continues, businesses and individuals have struggled with shutdowns, physical distancing, supply chain disruptions, and unexpected shifts in work arrangements, as well as the pandemic's toll on physical and mental health. I've felt nearly all of this, and maybe you have too.

What happens in Minneapolis affects us all. In May 2020, in the United States, the murder of George Floyd, an unarmed African American man, at the hands of police, ignited intense demonstrations, which spread rapidly in shock waves around the world. This, and other unlawful police conduct that killed countless unarmed Black people, resulted in calls for defunding police departments and demands for change after centuries of racism. Some peaceful protests turned confrontational and extended beyond demands for police reform to calls for removal of monuments and landmarks that are symbols of imperialist power, violence, and racial terror.

During this time, many people in the United States—and perhaps the world—realized that the exhaustion, anxiety, and ambiguity within themselves might be related to the persistent inequity and anxiety they see around them in society. You, like them, might be asking how—through inaction, silence, distraction, or dodging what feels complicated and uncomfortable—you have contributed consciously or unconsciously to the perpetuation of systemic racial injustice and to the global climate crisis. These questions ask for a different, more soulful, wholehearted, all-in engagement. Again, I kept asking myself, "Where is hope now?"

After months of wrestling with this question without answers, I resolved that maybe there weren't answers. Honestly, I felt hopeless, but the question kept lingering in me.

The following year, in 2021, I tiptoed into the online dating world, knowing I wasn't ready, but I would let hope lead me anyway. Is there a way to enter into a relationship without the risk of having your heart broken? I don't think so. I was vulnerable, maybe too vulnerable, too fragile, and I got dumped twice by the same guy. Where is hope now? It has taken much longer than I would have wanted to make sense of what was happening to and around me. I don't have answers, and the question of hope persists.

In September 2021, perhaps fed by climate crisis, a record-setting storm, Hurricane Ida, destroyed a part of my house. I was dazed and running on pure adrenaline as I worked with disaster volunteers to shovel and haul bags of mud out the basement—mud that was left behind when a six-foot wall of water wiped out the furnace, electrical panel, and water heater, and then ripped through the kitchen, trashing much of the first floor. After months of working with contractors to restore my house, in December 2021, I received a call in the middle of the night that my brother Milton, who had been hospitalized for weeks, had gone into septic shock. I had better come now, the caller said. I got on a plane the next day and arrived at the hospital just before he was taken into emergency surgery to amputate his leg, which was the result of medical complications, including renal disease.

As a Buddhist, I have learned and lived a basic premise: life contains suffering. I've trained and even taken a vow to face the truth of suffering, to see and accept reality as it is while holding the aspiration to work for a more compassionate, peaceful, and just world. Inherently, hope carries with it the possibility that we may not get what we hoped for—the job, the partner, the house, whatever—which carries with it the potential for suffering: fear, anxiety, and disappointment.

Hope is not about swinging between optimism and pessimism. Again, the desire for things to be other than what they are is said to be the root of suffering. This isn't a somber recognition but a capacity to hold the truth of our lives, whether that reality is painful or pleasurable. I've been atomized, deconstructed by the painful losses, the complications I've described. And I am called to awaken to a basic truth: whether hope is there or not, I must live from my deeply held values of simplicity, awakening, and peace, and let that be my guide.

This approach powerfully aligns with the work of Joanna Macy, a scholar of Buddhism, general systems theory, and deep ecology. In her book *Active Hope*, Macy speaks of passive and active hope. Passive hope is about "waiting for external agencies to bring about what we desire. Active hope is about becoming active participants in bringing about what we hope for."[2] Active hope is powered by our intention, and Macy describes a clear process of cultivating active hope. First, we take a "clear view of reality," again echoing the Buddhist teachings on seeing reality as it is. Second, we identify a direction or our value that we want to see expressed, and third, we take action to move in that direction. For Macy, active hope doesn't require optimism, so we can cultivate it even when we feel hopeless. Rather than weighing our chances and moving forward only if we feel hopeful, we allow our intention, our aspiration, and our purpose to guide our actions and focus instead on choosing to act in alignment with these values.

Building on Macy's principles of active hope, Buddhist teacher Roshi Joan Halifax speaks of wise hope "born of radical uncertainty, rooted in the unknown and the unknowable. . . . Wise hope requires that we open ourselves to what we do not know, what we cannot know; that we open ourselves to being surprised, perpetually surprised. In fact, wise hope appears through the spaciousness of radical uncertainty, of surprise, and this is the space in which we can engage."[3] It's in not knowing that "hope comes alive." It's in our capacity to see things as they are and to believe that our actions matter even if we don't know, can't know the outcome. We are guided by what we care about, what matters most to us, and what we can do to support healing within ourselves and in our beautiful and broken world. Trust and courage are active components of wise hope, echoed in the now-famous words of the former Czech statesman Václav Havel, who said, "Hope is definitely not the same thing as optimism. It is not the conviction that something will turn out well but the certainty that something makes sense, regardless of how it turns out."

When I consider the question I have asked myself these last several years—Where is hope now?—I return to the Buddhist principle of interconnectedness. What happens to me affects you; what happens to you affects me. With this, I realize I am not alone. We all have some measure of suffering and satisfaction. It's inescapable.

This book is a response to the question "Where is hope now?" I don't know, can't know how things will turn out, but I do know that the process of asking myself this question, of staying true to the mystery of this interconnectedness, of recognizing that love is deeply connected to loss, and of living in service of creating a more compassionate life even when compassion seems very far away is an important intention, value, and direction.

Immense and rapid change is under way and hardwired in daily life. There are no quick-fix solutions to loss of soul, loss of meaning and purpose, loss of hope, racial and social injustice, and climate crisis. Resistance, inertia, confusion, and fear of change are giving way to calls for reflection, courage, and action with purpose and intention. As individuals and as a global community, we are moving into something much larger and deeper. In some ways, this time of global disruption and personal crisis is like following a trackless path or sliding down a hill, losing my footing over and over again as I try to make sense of these profound shifts that have shaped my becoming.

We are being called to braver things, to lean forward into hope and action. Despite it all, choosing hope feels right, makes sense. It's true I didn't ask for this mess of losses, complications, and challenges. But at some point, recognizing that loss, that woundedness is a part of life as risk is a part of love, leads me to choose hope as a way of connecting with everyone else who knows about loss and love, and it leads me toward a more soul-filled and hope-filled life. Hope is the resolve to live with a generous heart, to dedicate and rededicate myself, to awaken my soul's voice at this sacred time of global disruption.

This call to bravery, to hope, isn't a book I want to write; it's a book I am called to write. All my life, and especially these most recent years, I've navigated scary places, cycles of disruption, and grief. Yet I hold the inner knowing that life is beautiful and that brokenness is essential to wholeness. This is something worth sharing. This is a book about small and sometimes less-small practices that can lead to a bold and brave life. It reads partly as a memoir, partly as a guidebook with lots of practices that you can use every day, and partly as a story-book illuminated by people filled with hope.

* * *

The internal disruption of emotional and spiritual alienation and uncertainty is not uncommon. "For many years, I read much and understood nothing," writes Teresa of Avila[4]. And the Buddhist teacher Pema Chodron writes, "We will be softened by the sheer force of whatever energy arises: the energy of anger, the energy of disappointment, the energy of fear."[5] Early Quaker George Fox brings another perspective; he spoke of "two thirsts": to find comfort and security in created things and to find that same comfort in the Creator.[6] Even throughout this time of tumultuous crisis, I was drawn forward toward making conscious and intentional my soul's voice, even while feeling uncertain. A lot wasn't clear, but what was clear was that I was moving toward the One True Thing: my soul.

Often individuals and groups—mentees and coachees, retreatants and pilgrims, religious—reach out to me with quite legitimate questions about the state of their soul, their inner being. They often want straightforward, ready-made answers that will awaken their own intuitive guidance or help them distinguish the inner critic from the voice of the inner soul friend. They want help addressing the tension of years, perhaps decades, of unspoken conflict within their institutions, hoping to resolve issues without the people involved taking legitimate risk. I don't have answers. I'm not checking in as an expert. What I am is grateful for the abundant guidance I receive from all directions: from the natural environment, from the "mistakes" that led me to the center of my being, and from all kinds of people, some of whom you'll meet in this book.

Often, I stand at the edge of clear sight, facing a hard truth. I'm asked to create a vision of myself that is larger and more expansive than I could imagine. My insecurities and uncertainties don't disappear. Instead, they demand attentiveness to my life patterns and choices, to listening that becomes a way of praying not for goods or services but for openness and bravery, to returning, always returning to what matters most.

I have a daily practice of asking myself, "Am I rationalizing, ignoring, sidestepping a voice that is struggling to be heard, calling me to be more generous, more loving, braver?" On this sense of living with intention, value, and purpose, the writer Rebecca Solnit has said, "Every minute of every hour of every day, you are making the world just as you are making yourself and you might as well do it with generosity and kindness and style."[7]

The cultural anthropologist Angeles Arrien found that in many shamanic societies and among many Indigenous elders, if you came to a shaman complaining of being disheartened, dispirited, or depressed, they would ask one of four questions: "When did you stop dancing?" "When did you stop singing?" "When did you stop being enchanted by stories?" and "When did you stop being comforted by the sweet territory of silence?"[8]

So I ask you: Are you dancing, singing, storytelling, silent enough? This book is an invitation to listen to silence, to tell your story, to notice patterns, and to actively, wisely choose hope.

Navigating This Book

Sail with me. Let this book guide you:

- Embark on life's essential questions of true aliveness and meaning.

- Discover greater bravery and courage when you're broken, uncomfortable, hammered, or hurt by life.

- Cultivate clarity and discernment that leads toward your authentic self.

With this book as your companion on your brave journey leaning toward hope, you will find features and content that provide structure and offer practices for growth. Each chapter explores one of Buddhism's Seven Factors of Awakening: mindfulness, investigation, energy, joy, tranquility, concentration, and equanimity. These might sound like lofty ideals; however, they refer to a set of embodied practices readily available to all of us. By using this frame, we explore aspects of awakening essential to growth.

Within each chapter is a section titled "Real Voices, Real Courage," highlighting one person's story of their commitment to living bravely, intentionally, and generously. Each of these cameos is followed by guided mindfulness practices in the Plum Village tradition of Zen master Thich Nhat Hanh. At the end of each chapter is a list of Quaker-style "queries." This is a spiritual practice among members of the Religious Society of Friends in the form of questions for spiritual discernment and reflection designed to strengthen capacity to align action toward a life of love and spirit. As you enter the queries, it's important to remember they don't have right-or-wrong, yes-or-no answers. Instead, engaging them is a spiritual discipline, a practice that can lead to new action and new ways of thinking. These queries serve a critical role in the spiritual life of Friends because Quakers don't have creeds or formal statements of beliefs. Instead of a creed, Quakers ascribe to a continuing relationship with God, or the Inward Light, that reveals truth and prompts action. Quakers call this relationship with God "ongoing revelation," historically referred to as "continuing revelation." Many Friends don't have ministers or clergy, believing that each person holds "that of God" within and therefore has direct, unmediated contact with this Divine Presence, so ministers or priests aren't required to intercede.

Rich in Buddhist and Quaker spiritual wisdom and practice, *Hope Leans Forward* is also meant to be a "play" book, designed to be held lightheartedly. As you read and engage the practices, don't press yourself to "get it right." Instead, let it surprise, inspire, and warm your heart, and then see where that leads you. Listen and know that your heart has the genuine strength and beauty to meet you where you are, to grow and to flourish especially when times are tough.

Decisive moments—heartbreak moments—shape and reshape a life of truth seeking. Paradoxically, these are turning points that also awaken the soul, the True Self, to hold true to the vision of who you are while honoring who you are becoming. Remember, you are the courage you are seeking. Let it rediscover you. Let *Hope Leans Forward* be your return-to guidebook as your soul awakens, which means whatever you learn in these pages, you likely need to relearn again and again. This is an invitation to start now.

I've found a lot of unexpected, unplanned beauty in "getting lost," in making the "wrong turn" that led me down a path to an unexpected treasure: the gnarly, venerable apple tree loaded with fruit, the person harvesting grapes in the field, or the stranger with a lovely smile that draws us together for an moment of connection. Allow your own instinct, your intuition, to guide you as you read. You are beginning to learn to trust this perhaps-hidden part of yourself. To give you a sense of how the book will unfold, the courage, the practices, and the challenges, the following pages offer a short introduction to each chapter. Again, whatever you read or however you read the materials, trust what is truest for *you*.

Chapter 1, Calling the Soul, the True Self, and the Deepest Longing

It's hard to break the cycle of habitual patterns and move toward bravery without awakening. Waking the psyche or soul, the inner voice, to deeper awareness, is a lifelong practice. Awakening the soul, the True Self, is about pausing and slowing down to listen and ask important questions of life meaning, purpose, and aliveness. It's about recognizing and honoring the life you have while holding the vision of the life you want. The soul is seeking to make visible our intention and purpose. Awakening the soul, the True Self, also involves engaging the dismal, the unfulfilled, the too-much life cycles, which takes courage. In this chapter, the first of the Seven Factors of Awakening is mindfulness. The "Real Voices, Real Courage" cameo comes from my conversation with eli tizcareño, urban farmer. The mindfulness practice is awareness of the breath, based on the Buddhist sutra on the Full Awareness of Breathing, followed by a short form of mindful breathing to strengthen awareness and calm the body and mind.

Chapter 2, Daring to Listen to the Inner Voice, the Small Holy

Once the soul has awakened—through loss, grief, a birth or death, nature, a new insight, a relationship, a job loss or gain, and more—it extends the invitation to listen in a new and different way. As we listen, we learn to distinguish the small holy, the soul voice, from the voice of the often-robust Inner Critic. In this chapter, the reader is introduced to the second of the Seven Factors of Awakening: investigation. "Real Voices, Real Courage" presents the thoughts of LoAn Nguyen, trans rights advocate. The mindfulness practice is deep listening for resonance, with an open mind and open heart.

Chapter 3, When Life Breaks You Open: Practice and Growth

As we begin to acknowledge and take responsibility for and good care of the soul voice, we may be confronted with a primal anxiety, inner tensions, complexity and chaos, and "shadow" elements that offer a way forward into the Mystery of the soul.

Among the things that confront us are new questions we might ask: How does the broken heart become the fertile ground of new vitality? How can you hold a broken heart? The reader is introduced to the third of the Seven Factors of Awakening: energy. The "Real Voices, Real Courage" cameo in this chapter is about George Lakey, a Quaker activist. The mindfulness practice is handling strong emotions.

Chapter 4, Trusting True Self: Taking the Risk to Blossom

Finding meaning and learning to trust ourselves and to risk vulnerability in the inevitable cycles of anguish, betrayal, guilt, and self-doubt—the dismal places—are in part the journey of the soul toward greater resilience, bravery, and an inner aliveness. This chapter focuses on practices that support building trust, bravery, and resilience, and the reader is introduced to the fourth of the Seven Factors of Awakening: joy. The "Real Voices, Real Courage" section features Susan Cross, craftswoman and ceremonialist, and the mindfulness practice in this chapter is cultivating joy.

Chapter 5, Cultivating Wholeness: The Body as Grounded Wisdom

Too often, we're cut off from the wisdom of the body. We've learned to rely heavily on what the rational mind can perceive or stumble over, barely aware of the body's need for rest and renewal and its capacity to guide us with grounded, body-centered wisdom. This chapter introduces the reader to the fifth of the Seven Factors of Awakening: tranquility. "Real Voices, Real Courage" in this chapter spotlights Brian Braganza, facilitator and change maker. The mindfulness practice is the body scan, cultivating awareness of the various parts and the wholeness of the body to restore calm and renewal.

Chapter 6, Deepening Connections: Journeying with Community, Mentors, and Friends

The ability to establish and maintain healthy and supportive relationships with diverse individuals and groups is a critical part of the ongoing journey to live bravely. None of us can go it alone. We need authentic connections to help us create the person we wish to become. Living bravely requires the kind of honesty that is fostered within a compassionate community and among trusted friends and mentors. In this chapter, the reader is introduced to the sixth of the Seven Factors of Awakening, concentration, and in "Real Voices, Real Courage," we'll meet Francisco Burgos, the executive director of the Pendle Hill Quaker retreat and study center. The mindfulness practice is beginning anew, a process of reconciliation in community and between individuals. (As a note to readers, I founded and led the Journey Toward Wholeness program for many years at Pendle Hill.)

Chapter 7, Living Your Genuine: Truth Telling to Embrace the True Self

As we deepen our connection to our body and to trusted friends and allies, we begin to discern how to live with the bravery, beauty, and vulnerability that are present always. The reader is introduced to the seventh of the Seven Factors of Awakening: equanimity. The cameo portrait in "Real Voices, Real Courage" is of Fanny Brewster, Jungian analyst. The mindfulness practice is touching the earth—a nourishing, contemplative practice that calms and grounds an overstimulated body and mind.

Chapter 8, Bravely Home: Boundless Joy (Well, Maybe Basic Okayness) on the Way Back to You

We learn a lot by embracing the fullness of our own beauty and vulnerability when we welcome a boundless heart and meet ourselves in new, fresh, and joyful ways. This chapter celebrates that new meeting by integrating learning, visioning possibility, and leaning into action courageously. "Real Voices, Real Courage" features Ilana Kaufman, executive director of the Jews of Color Initiative. The mindfulness practice is mindful walking, which intentionally cultivates awareness in movement.

Now that You've Set Sail, Let the Wind Be at Your Back: Ways to Engage This Book

This book is meant to be like a glide in a sailboat along a gentle current. As you sail along, you might stop, fascinated by a bird call, and listen. Perhaps you will turn into a deserted cove and anchor for a while, taking in the moment. You're not in a hurry to get somewhere. You're here, just here, and that's more than enough, for now. And that feels good, you notice.

While you read this book as though sailing on that gentle current, allow yourself to be caught by delight, by surprise, by wonder. Discover something new about yourself. As you move through the book, consider this a reading meditation, an opportunity to practice mindfulness. Read and reread passages. Slow down the pace. Look around. Smell the salty air. Allow the spacious sky overhead to be your teacher. Learn something. Relearn something. Unlearn something. And then do it all over again and again.

Since we're on this journey together, it's useful to have some shared understandings as we navigate each chapter together. I list a few offerings for ways to begin. Better still, create your own navigational tools for how best to be with this book journey.

Acknowledge the Land Ancestors

Land acknowledgments have become ubiquitous. Sometimes they feel perfunctory, almost singsongy, losing their connection to people and place. Land is in us. We are the land. The land is our history and carries stories of colonialism, imperialism, forced migration, and enslavement, as well as stories of communion, nourishment, birth, love, play, death, and so much more. Land acknowledgments make space for this reality.

My feet are touching the earth in New Hope, Pennsylvania, the territorial homelands of the Lenni Lenape Nation, and specifically an area called Aquetong, which means "spring in the bushes." Take a moment to recognize and to acknowledge the native people who inhabited the land upon which you are now situated. You might find the Native Land Digital online map (https://native-land.ca) a useful guide to find the names of those people.

Kindness First

Be kind to yourself. Take your time. There is no need to rush through this to get to another place, to find something you don't already know about yourself. Kindness also means caring not only for your emotions and spirit but also for your body. Move in a way that is supportive. If you find that you're sitting hunchbacked over the book, stop, move, breathe. Put the book down and take good care of yourself. When you've done that, return.

You're Enough; This Moment Is Enough

You're here because someone loved and cared enough. Perhaps not perfectly, and not in the way you wanted and needed, but someone cared enough. Remember that. Remember what enough looks like. You may not have everything figured out at the end of this book, and that's okay. Let something new arise for you, and let that be enough—for now.

Pause, Relax, Open, Trust Emergence, Listen Deeply, Speak the Truth

This book asks you to look deeply into your life, and that's not always easy. Insight Dialogue is a modern practice developed in the 1980's and 1990's by Buddhist teacher Gregory Kramer. It offers useful guidance on how to move the practice of meditation from the cushion into speaking and listening that itself is a form of meditation. The basic guidance is to pause, relax, open, trust emergence, listen deeply, and speak the truth.[9] I offer this as a framework for how to engage this book, and you'll engage more with this in chapter 2. As you read, pause when you come to a sentence, paragraph, or page that speaks to you. Allow your body to relax as you hold this book in your hands. Notice where you might hold tension and gently soften. Open yourself to whatever truth you find in these pages, even hard truths—maybe especially hard truths. Trust that you already have everything you need and that whatever emerges is okay for now. Listen for nudges and leanings that might ignite an inner knowing, and then speak that as your truth.

Find a Reading Partner

As you read this book and work through the meditations and reflections, don't go it alone. Connect with another person—a trusted friend, spiritual friend, or group of people who also want to explore braving your way toward simplicity, awakening, and peace. In the Plum Village tradition, we know that individual transformation is inseparable from collective transformation. We have a practice called The Second Body, which engages the support of another person to accompany us physically, emotionally, and spiritually, and that engagement magnifies our awareness. To transform, we need the love, support, and understanding of others. Seek out those people, and practice reading this book together as a community.

Try "Yes, and" Thinking

One of the basic tenets of improv comedy is "Yes, and." It's a protocol that allows for anything to happen, and it goes like this: No matter what your fellow actors present to you, instead of negating it, belittling it, or disagreeing with it, you say, "Yes, and—." Accept the scenario as it's presented to you (regardless of where you wanted it to go), and then add to it. Volley back with something your fellow players can respond to. "Yes, and" thinking is jet fuel for creativity and collaboration. It is about accepting and expanding what's been offered. Although you might not agree with everything written here, what if, while reading this book, you practiced "Yes, and" thinking and held it with openness and a willingness to shift your views?

Engage the Seventh Generation Principle

The Seventh Generation Principle is based on an ancient Haudenosaunee (Iroquois) philosophy that the decisions we make today should result in a sustainable world seven generations into the future.[10] The Seventh Generation Principle states that decisions made about energy, water, and natural resources should ensure that they are sustainable for seven generations into the future from the present point. Applying this principle to relationships, the intention is that every decision should result in sustainable relationships up through seven generations. As you read this book, consider how your actions today might affect others far into the future. Pause and reflect on the living legacy you want others in future generations to recall about how you lived into acts of bravery and courage. Consider the legacy you are creating for the future by the choices you make today. Choose love.

One Size Doesn't Fit Everyone: Meditation Is Person and Context Specific

Mindfulness meditation in the Plum Village tradition has greatly supported and benefited me in gaining insights, addressing emotional and psychological states, and creating greater well-being. It's the meditation community, tradition, and practice I am most familiar with, and I refer to it extensively in this book and in my work and life. My mindfulness practice is part of an overall personal plan of well-being that includes psychotherapy, regular medical care, and alternative and complementary care, like yoga, massage, chiropractic, and acupuncture treatments, as well as regular support of a mentor, an experienced Plum Village Dharma teacher, a support group for Dharma teachers, and regular one-on-one peer conversations with other Dharma teachers.

There are now decades of research celebrating the numerous benefits of mindfulness meditation and meditation generally. Yet even meditation may not be 100 percent safe for all people all the time. Rather than a one-size-fits-all approach to meditation, consider your own personal history and context and feel empowered to choose what is appropriate for you.

Mindfulness meditation is person- and context-centered, meaning that it's important for you as the reader to take into account your own personal context, circumstances, history of trauma, social support and social connection, and emotional, physical, and psychological states.

Mindfulness meditation should above all do no harm. It should be safe. Yet there is significant research that speaks to meditation-related distress for some meditators. A good resource for beginning to explore the challenging, difficult, and potentially distressing effects of meditation is Brown University's Varieties of Contemplative Experience research project.[11] To get support if you experience meditation-related distress, consider reaching out to Cheetah House (www.cheetahhouse.org).

Chapter 1

CALLING THE SOUL, THE TRUE SELF, AND THE DEEPEST LONGING

"The soul," I said, "was the one who just answered the question 'Why are you really here?' It is the wise and whole and brave part of the self. The soul is the ageless longing for truth that sends scientists into the lab and seekers onto the spiritual path."

—Elizabeth Lesser[1]

Howard Thurman, one of the most prominent theologians of the twentieth century, was born with a caul, an intact amniotic sac covering him in a sheath, a soft bubble. His newborn face, masked by the caul, was protected first within the womb and then outside his mother's body. Every culture has its folklore about these rare and mysterious en caul births, about their meaning and power. In African American culture, it is said that to be born "behind the veil" is both a blessing and a curse, conveying second sight, or the power of clairvoyance. Those given this gift and curse may also be given sad and grief-stricken lives. To lose the caul, with its gift and curse, one has to pierce the ears of the newborn to deflate the caul, though even that doesn't entirely eliminate the power of the veil.

As a young boy, Thurman discovered a bit of scar tissue in the middle of each earlobe. He asked his mother and grandmother, a skilled midwife who had formerly been enslaved for twenty-two years, what the scars meant. The women told him about the veil, its power and peril, and why they had pierced his ears. Thurman's peculiar birth set the tone for his soul-centered life. Not only was he a theologian by training, he was also a mystic from birth, and his lifelong work explored the depth of soul making. In his writing and teaching, in his speeches and lectures, he wove together the spiritual, intellectual, and emotional with clarity and meaning. He continually asked himself hope-filled questions, "What is most genuine? What is waiting within? How shall I listen? Where am I being called?"

Thurman's life and legacy centered on an inward search of the soul that led to an outward expression in his work and actions. His search for soul making was found in silence and solitude, in engagement and action. He modeled a way of understanding the mystery of the human soul.

It's impossible to adequately describe the soul, to capture its exact meaning. I can write about Thurman's soulwork and can speak about my experience of listening, sensing, dodging, bargaining, ignoring, and cultivating the landscape within and how I came to understand soul making within me. As you read this, even with definitions that are hard to capture, listen and notice whatever arises within you, and ask yourself, "How is soul making expressed in my life?"

Naming the Soul

Soul making, listening to the call of the soul, is at the center of being human. And this call is something we are invited to feel from all the corners of our life: mind, body, spirit, emotions, and identity. The soul is a place of mystery, depth, and genuineness that is described by many names, such as True Self, Inner Wisdom, Essential Self, Inner Teacher, Inward Teacher, Inward Light, and others. The soul is known in many cultures, genders, ethnic groups, geographic regions, and spiritual and religious traditions and faiths.

When I speak of soul, I am not referring to intellect or willpower, though to engage the soul may be to touch these aspects of the human experience. Writer and educator Parker Palmer has said that the soul "points toward a mystery for which nobody has the true name or the real story. Every tradition has a name for it; it is the *being* in *human being*. What a person calls it doesn't matter to me, but *that* we call it something matters a lot."[2]

I learned about soul making, about hope and bravery at a young age. Completely unprepared and uncertain for what was ahead, I left home at eighteen after my mother's early and sudden death. She had been my primary caretaker after my father left the family very early on, and I loved her with all my heart. The wake of her death left me emotionally broken. How could I go on? Who would guide me? What life could I create for myself without her?

Dazed and scared as I was when I left, I took very little with me—some clothes and a few dolls, which I wrapped in a sheet and threw in the back of my boyfriend's pickup—and hit the road. The pain of leaving behind many meaningful possessions, such as the beautiful Vietnamese doll from my brother's tour of duty and my favorite sweater, stayed with me for many years. I left home and started my journey to find the sacred center—a new home, my place of belonging in a complex world—without a guidebook, compass, or map.

At first, I searched for a sense of home, for a place of belonging, by trying to prove my worthiness through unrelenting, exhausting work to get out of poverty and obtain an education. The search took me through college, graduate school, and law school. As I built a narrow, well-ordered life, I lost myself again and again in the ambition, the race to succeed in my career. I kept looking over my shoulder, though, terrified that I would lose everything I had worked so single-mindedly to acquire. I thought financial stability and a successful career would make my life meaningful. I substituted a career for a life of connectedness and belonging. I forgot, or perhaps never learned, how to *be* in the world, how to listen to myself and others, how to love and feel fully alive. All the while, my sense of incompleteness, a sense that something important was missing, persisted.

Because I was on the run from myself, from my emotions, from risking connections, I hid myself from my friends, relations, and colleagues with a measured, arm's-length distance that I thought would keep me safe and out of emotional harm's way. But the strategy backfired. I found that in not authentically sharing myself with others, in hiding myself, I cut myself off from the potential of meaningful relationships. Trying to outdistance vulnerability, I also outdistanced love and belonging. Living emotionally distant from myself reinforced an emotional boundary, a high wall of separation that at first felt safe and then, over time, became a prison. I hid behind this wall, pretending that everything was all right, knowing that it wasn't.

As I began to follow the thread of distancing myself back to where it all began, I realized that this sense of separation started with messages from my early childhood, like "Don't depend on anyone" and "Be independent." These messages were meant to encourage me to be strong, safe, and independent, especially as a young Black person, but when overused, they trapped me. I was so strong, so independent, so competent; I needed so little from anyone. Yet I could not think my way over the divide I had created. I had to find another way.

Then everything changed in a moment when I knew I was deeply lost to an essential part of myself and needed to find a way back to what I had never fully trusted or acknowledged: my inner voice, my soul. In the mid-1990s, after a particularly stressful time at work, I decided to go on a hiking vacation in one of my favorite places in New Mexico. I climbed to the top of a big hill and took off my backpack. Looking up, I saw the clouds drift slowly across the sky. Stunned, I sat there, hearing myself say, "Is this what clouds do? How is it that I never noticed? Where was I? What was I hurrying to that I missed this?"

At that moment, I knew I was not only alienated from the natural world; I was alienated from myself. Looking up at the sky and *really* seeing the clouds, without having to *get* or *prove* anything, without having to *earn the right* to linger in the moment, without having finished all the projects waiting on my to-do list, without feeling driven to rush to the next thing, was the soul practice that began to guide me intuitively back home to myself.

Years later, I would stumble across this poem by the poet Gregory Orr, which captures that profound moment. Orr says,

Has the moon been up there
All these nights
And I never noticed?

A whole week with my nose
To the ground, to the grind.

And the beloved faithfully
Returning each evening
As the moon.

Where have I been?
Who has abandoned whom?[3]

As this fledging intuition to reconnect with a part of myself that was hard to see and understand grew stronger, I began a search to find my True Self, my soul, which led me on a decades-long journey of spiritual exploration. Earlier, in my early twenties, I had turned away from Catholicism—the religion I was born and raised into, the religion of my mother and grandmother—and began a rambling search across the world for a spiritual home that continued throughout my thirties and forties.

Diving into spiritual practices to awaken the wild and untamed parts of my soul that were squashed by my uber sense of responsibility and fear led me to far-off places. I enrolled in courses on forgiveness, active listening, authentic movement, and improv. At the same time in my twenties, I began making solo pilgrimages around the world. In my thirties, after traveling to Asia and India on multiple trips, I turned toward Buddhism and specifically to Thich Nhat Hanh and the Plum Village community, at first out of curiosity and to relieve stress and then as place of healing. I kept exploring, which led me to Ethical Humanism. Though I appreciated the community, my heart was calling for a soft aliveness that wasn't there for me in the rationality of Ethical Humanism. By chance in 1999, I began studying Kundalini yoga, which gave me a more holistic view of myself. Instead of perceiving my body as an assemblage of unrelated functional parts, I came to appreciate a core awareness and aliveness.

These multiple faiths and practices shaped my views of God, Spirit, and soul. I'm aware, too, that the words *God*, *Spirit*, and *soul* have many meanings. It's important for everyone who does this work to come to their own definition, their own understanding of these words. Like nested woven baskets, each faith and practice I engaged felt supported by the others. Today, I hold both Buddhist and Quaker faith and practice, and my life and work, my soul, is anchored by Kundalini yoga and pilgrimage journeys. I bring from Quaker tradition an understanding of soul as referring to the Inner or Inward Light of God. And as a Buddhist, I understand soul as Buddha nature, the deepest part of being human, the True Self.

All the spiritual work and exploration I was doing over many years cracked me open to vulnerability, and I sensed a new possibility that laid the formative ground for growth in courage, hope, and bravery. As vulnerable as I was, I kept taking leaps of faith, testing my courage, and sinking into uncertainty and doubt. With each new spiritual exploration, I was drawn into self-discovery, mystery, and wide-open risk. Each time I embraced a new faith and practice or explored a different part of the world on a solo pilgrimage, I experienced hesitation and dark clouds of doubt all over again, yet I knew I was being called to an open sea, toward a more authentic version of myself, toward this sense of soul.

Soul Formation: My Early Years

My early family years in Brooklyn formed my soul, leading me on a seeker's journey to law school, across the world, and back home again in a new and different way. For me, that place and my parents were an important, early part of my understanding of the call of soul.

I was raised by fearless Black people; my Cuban mother and Jamaican father and relatives gave me an early appreciation of the world as a large and complex place. They were hard-working people. And like many people who immigrate, they were caught in a sort of assimilationist limbo. Having left their native Caribbean lands, they no longer belonged to their old homelands, yet they were not integrated into this American culture. Their arduous journey to the United States from their island countries was full of possibility and peril, not unlike a pilgrim's journey. With little more than a suitcase, they came bearing the collective consciousness of their ancestors—their parents and their parents' parents—as pilgrims who travel with a sense of *communitas*, a quality of togetherness, a shared encounter. Perhaps most of all, my parents came with hope. Hope was by their side as they made plans. Hope inspired their vision. Hope colored their motivation.

They had to navigate so many unknowns that could have kept them immobilized and small in an unfamiliar land with its customs, culture, language, and food, but they entered with hope and bravery. In her essay "The Place Beyond Fear and Hope," the writer Margaret Wheatley says, "Hope never enters the room without fear at its side."[4]

Like those on a long pilgrimage with a clear destination in mind, my parents undertook a journey of hardship, uncertainty, and insecurity. Along the way, they learned from the journey, allowing it to shape their beautiful and terrifying voyage into the unknown. Fear and insecurity often provide energy, tools to figure things out along the way, and so it was for my parents—and now is for me.

My soul making began with instability, fear, and insecurity. My parents separated early on, after pressures of trying to fit into life in New York City made their marriage more painful and turbulent. Growing up amid poverty and violence, I carried the weight of my mother's sacrifice. She, as a single parent, worked as a maid at the Hotel Manhattan to support my three brothers and me after my father had largely disappeared from the family and my life. Unprepared and blurry eyed from too much happening too soon, I left home at eighteen, two years after my mother's unexpected death.

I searched for a sense of home, a sense of belonging. Ultimately, this search became a search for soul. I got a job at Burger King and went to City University of New York at night through a special program that allowed anyone who graduated from high school in New York City to enter college free of cost. I jumped on the opportunity to receive an academic scholarship to graduate school and then law school, believing that as a lawyer I would find belonging in the safety and security of a job with benefits and middle-class status—the life my parents had hoped for. With an academic scholarship, I entered law school at Howard, a historically Black university in Washington, DC, during the time of the great civil rights leaders like Justice Thurgood Marshall, Julian Bond, and James Baldwin, who were frequent visitors to the school. They instilled in me and other law students big aspirations of social justice, self-worth, and self-love. I graduated law school with these aspirations. Then when I submerged myself in my Big and Important Job as a lawyer-lobbyist, I lost the aspirations. I wanted to do good, to have my mother's sacrifice amount to something, to have her proud of me. My life wouldn't be defined by a life of struggle, a low-paying, thankless job.

Trying to prove myself, live into my mother's hopes, her unlived life, I rushed constantly. I hardly took in a full breath, and I nursed a fragile security as I climbed the ladder of success. Each step on the rung was a way to control and make predictable an earlier life born from chaos.

I absorbed middle-class values and status symbols and spent years trying to measure up and fit in. Straightening my hair, I mastered fitting into white culture, silencing myself so others could feel comfortable. In doing so, I forgot all the ways my soul speaks, how to listen deeply to myself and others, how to love and be loved, how to rest, how to be tender with myself and with others. I forgot how to feel fully alive.

But my soul continued to search, to speak. Even before law school, while I was in undergraduate school, I heard the voice of my soul calling. My soul search brought me to unlikely places high above sea level in the desert mountains, in the rugged canyons and mesas of the painted desert of northern New Mexico.

I went to Ghost Ranch, made famous by the artist Georgia O'Keeffe, where I arrived with a hurry-up, city-folk mindset. My soul gasped for air, and at the ranch, I finally found a way to breathe. Pulling into the ranch's dirt and gravel road on the back of my boyfriend's motorcycle, I instantly fell in love with the land and the vast sky of the ranch. The boyfriend moved on to other things, but the love I found for the ranch endured. I entered a totally unfathomable world that was so unlike anything I knew or understood.

My time exploring the dusty back roads of northern New Mexico stayed with me, and over many years throughout my thirties, forties, and fifties, I would return to the ranch as a place to recover a sense of soul—first as a visitor, then as a farmhand planting forty pounds of garlic, one clove at a time, and later as a retreat leader and sojourner. As a farmhand, I learned to braid softneck garlic and to grind Hopi blue corn. I worked the land each day, bending low toward the ground, feeling the crumbling red clay soil between my fingers, walking the rows of garlic and heirloom corn in the shadow of Pedernal, the blue-black mesa towering over the ranch. There I studied herbs with a *curandera*, learning the healing properties of the land itself. Instinctively, I knew I was finding a part of myself, my soul.

Breathing in the scent of piñon and sage at Ghost Ranch, I knew each time I returned that this place retrieved an essential part of me. Something lush and uncharted awakened in me and was changed forever. The poet Mark Nepo writes that each person is born with an "unencumbered spot . . . an umbilical spot of grace where we were each first touched by God."[5] This is a part of each person that cannot be weighed or measured; it is a part of inner knowing, a beauty that sustains us.

Arriving at Ghost Ranch in my early thirties, lost in an inner wilderness of unprocessed anticipatory grief, ambiguous loss, and racialized trauma, I was in between faiths. I was no longer practicing Catholicism, the faith of my mother and grandmother. At Ghost Ranch, which welcomes people of different faiths and traditions, cultures, genders, and ethnic groups, I knew I had come to the right place. I prayed, chanted, and danced with many of them. I lit Shabbat candles with Jewish friends, acknowledging *neshama* (soul) and *neshima* (breath). I practiced Kundalini yoga in a *gurdwara* with American Sikhs and rediscovered the importance of *seva*, selfless service. As I sat in silent prayer with Greek Orthodox monks or *kirtan* chanting with Hindus, each experience became soul expression. Each faith tradition offered a different insight into soul making. For Muslims, to express soul is to harmonize intention and actions toward God. From inter-spiritualists, soul making is drawing on the great wisdom of many traditions, distilling the essence of love. For Hindus, soul is a constant force within and around us. For Greek Orthodox Christians, soul making is expressed in prayer threaded throughout the day.

This immersion into different faiths led me to the Religious Society of Friends. By chance while on retreat at the ranch, I met a woman who was a longtime Quaker. When I told her of my search to find a spiritual home, she suggested I consider Friends. At the time I was living in Bucks County, Pennsylvania, surrounded by Quakers, though I didn't know it. When I returned home from the ranch, I visited the nearest Quaker meetinghouse and was immediately drawn by the sacred quiet, simplicity, and peace of the place. I had found soul.

I kept returning to the ranch from the 1990s through 2018, just before the start of the global pandemic, to remember what I had learned years earlier. Yet the hard-driving habits of a type A lawyer-lobbyist kept displacing the soul making. I was overwhelmed and trapped by my job, which paid all the bills but robbed me of a sense of soul and sense of self.

The stress took a toll on my health, leading to an unexpected surgery and the ending of my one-year tumultuous marriage when I was in my early thirties. After recovering from the surgery, I wanted to find what I thought I had lost in myself or never had, so I began to explore the world through solo pilgrimage to India, Asia, South America, the Pacific Islands, and Europe. I was totally clueless about the deeper spiritual significance of pilgrimage, yet I had my ancestors, my parents' determination, and a wayfarer's heart. As I encountered people of diverse cultures and backgrounds around the world, I began to see beyond the differences to what connected us. I found a universal love language of respect and kindness. I was learning something important about people and culture, and it was a gift I felt I needed to preserve and pass on.

Spirit was present in the street vendor selling chewing gum on the sidewalk in Quito, Ecuador. Compassion was alive at the standing crosses of the holy island of Iona in the Scottish Hebrides. Faith and inspiration were there in the beautifully complex dances of native Balinese people. So much was happening, and sometimes it felt like a jumble. I was working as a lawyer-lobbyist, traveling the world on solo pilgrimage often for a few weeks at a time, taking a brief time away from work, returning to Ghost Ranch, and exploring both Quakerism and mindfulness in the Plum Village tradition.

During this time of discovery and jumble, in 1995, my brother Trevor suggested I attend a public talk given by Thich Nhat Hanh at the Riverside Church in Manhattan. After I attended the talk, I found a local sangha, a Buddhist community, near my home. Some in the group were very experienced in Buddhism, and others, like me, were newbies. We met weekly at Rolling Green Farm, a historic property in New Hope, Pennsylvania. Our teachers and the sangha organizers were Zen poets/hippies and loved the Plum Village community. I fell in love too. When they decided to leave the farm to move to North Carolina, I moved into the farm to continue building the community. After a year of hauling firewood up and down stairs, trying to keep the stone house warm in the bitter and frozen cold, I moved out. But I didn't leave the practice of mindfulness or the Plum Village community. I joined the community and received the Five Mindfulness Trainings, Buddhist precepts for a life of well-being.

As my job became more and more stressful, my introduction to Buddhism became a source of internal support that helped me deal with the resulting burnout. The Buddhist path was so clear, offering me practical ways to calm my body and mind and to look deeply at patterns, habits, and beliefs. The Buddhist path looked like this:

- **Practice.** Though the path became clear, it wasn't easy, and I had a lot of unlearning to do. It was through the path of practice—of these *particular practices* I learned in the community—that my soul grew.

- **Recognition.** I learned to know what was happening around me and in me, and to see it clearly.

- **Acceptance.** I learned to accept whatever was happening in me and to give up fighting for things to be other than what they were or trying to muscle my way through. Acceptance was radical to me and gave me a kind of internal resting place.

- **Embrace.** I learned to bring forward the inherent energy of mindfulness that comes after acceptance. Embracing is grounded in kindness and compassion, love, and allowing that energy to hold whatever is there, especially holding the suffering. Just doing that helped me so much to find peace and self-acceptance.

- **Looking deeply.** In an overstimulated world, a skill I desperately needed was calming and soothing myself. With a degree of equanimity, calm, I could take a step back to understand what was happening to me and why. Looking deeply, I began to put the pieces of my life together, like filling in missing pieces of a massive jigsaw puzzle. Looking deeply, I started to understand why I chose to become a lawyer. Looking deeply, I recognized why I was driving myself so hard. I understood my fear and also the legacy of fear and suffering I had inherited from my parents and their parents.

- **Understanding and action.** It's said in Buddhism that the fruit of looking deeply is understanding or insight. I was beginning to understand the causes and conditions: my

> choices, how I was raised, why I became a
> lawyer, and more, which gave rise to insight,
> laying the foundation for experiencing the loss
> and the grief. But understanding is only part of
> this practice. The other part is taking skillful,
> compassionate, love-centered action.

This movement took many years of stopping and starting, of slowing myself down long enough to really recognize, accept, embrace, look deeply, and take action directed in love. This movement was not sequential, and it was what I continued practicing as I was breaking patterns—cycles driven not only by my own self-doubt and fear but also by societal norms and values of playing it safe, of making money and getting ahead, with the promise I'd be happy in some unknown future.

"Now to the Soul": Discovering Quaker Faith and Practice

After the encounter with the Quaker woman at Ghost Ranch and the public talk with Thich Nhat Hanh, around 2000, I went on retreat to Pendle Hill, the Quaker retreat and study center outside Philadelphia. My first retreat was a week of improvisational movement, a practice of free association of the body said to be a bridge between the conscious and unconscious.

I arrived at Pendle Hill's main gathering place, a converted milk barn, hoping that the exploration might open me up to something I could not yet articulate. There was stillness, community dialogue, and worship—a daily gathering of Quakers and non-Quakers for silent sitting with the Spirit, listening for Spirit-filled messages that are offered spontaneously by those present. I spent seven days bending, stretching, and rolling my body into one shape after another, sighing, rocking, and swaying until I felt different deep inside.

It wasn't what I had expected. The unexpected sense of safety and acceptance opened me up to a deeper part of myself. Feeling fluid, free, and unscripted in my body but mostly open to the presence of Mystery, I had discovered a way to listen to the call of soul through spiritual discernment, the heart of Quaker spirituality. Something stirred inside my bones and became an awakening as I realized that not just the mind but also the body held an intellect, a core awareness. My super serious, panic-driven life was pot-bound in the vessel of my body, which, like a plant that has outgrown its container, was too tight, too rigid to contain the suppleness of the soul. I was beginning to listen to the direction of my soul, to discern the path ahead.

Quaker writer Patricia Loring calls discernment a "central Quaker conviction of the availability to every person of the experience and guidance of God, immediate as well as mediated."[6] Spiritual discernment, she describes, is a "faculty" and "capacity" to know what is "of God" and what is not. It is a "fallible, intuitive gift we use in attempting to discriminate" when we are led by God or by "impulses" or "generalized judgments of conscience." Profoundly, Loring calls spiritual discernment a "gift from God, not a personal achievement," that is "not the result of training, technique, or analysis. Like other gifts of God, its origin is mysterious and gratuitous. It is given for the building of the community and of relationship with God rather than for self-fulfillment or self-aggrandizement." Discernment is part of a lifelong relationship with God where we learn to listen "to the profound and subtle and to let our lives speak."

After the retreat at Pendle Hill, I was drawn more deeply into Buddhist meditation practices, which complemented and strengthened my contemplative Quaker practices, especially as I participated in meeting for worship, writing, and reflecting on Quaker faith. As a way to understand both Quaker spirituality and Buddhist faith, I wrote essays on Buddhism and Quakerism for several Quaker magazines, offering how the faiths complement each other. Through Buddhism, I learned how to center in stillness and quiet the mind. In Quakerism, I was drawn closer to the Inward Light, my True Self, the call of soul.

The practices of soulwork, bodywork, and breathwork later led me to where I am today: a leadership coach, retreat leader, codirector at Georgetown University's Institute for Transformational Leadership, and chief mindfulness officer at my company, Lead Smart Coaching, where I meet people on a path of discernment, seeking to understand the call of the soul, seeking to recognize, accept, embrace, look deeply, and take action. They often turn to me after having lived with lots of hard shoulds and only-ifs, loaded with harsh self-critiques largely based on other people's values and regrets—a way of thinking that Jungian analyst Clarissa Pinkola Estés, in her book, *Women Who Run with the Wolves*, likens to "stuffing your soul with junk food."[7] They have lost touch with what is calling them toward an essential expression of their life and their purpose.

Many of us have a very loud inner critic. I like to call that voice the Little Stinker. For years, I tried hard to silence my inner critic—the voice that kept me on the run from myself, that kept me from truly connecting to my soul. Through Buddhism and Quakerism, I recognize that the Little Stinker is a part of me that needs lots of love, a warm embrace. On my better days, I'm able to offer that to myself as I see that even the Little Stinker is a part of my soul's work. I place a hand on my heart. I go for a walk along a creek. I look up at the sky and really see and feel the clouds. I allow for moments of mindfulness to soothe and calm me. From a more balanced emotional disposition, I have greater access to the big picture of my life and choose, again, in love, to embrace my soul's work and the practices from Buddhist and Quaker traditions that bring me to inner stillness and to the soul's opening.

We began this chapter with Howard Thurman's inspiring, soul-filled birth and life of continually returning to the voice of the genuine in his writing, his ministry, and his teaching. His life and legacy raise soul-filled questions, such as "What is most genuine? What is waiting within? How shall you listen? Where are you being called?"

SEVEN FACTORS OF AWAKENING: THE FIRST FACTOR, MINDFULNESS

Right Mindfulness is essential to Buddhist practice and is a whole-body-and-mind awareness of the present moment. Mindfulness incorporates several elements:

- Paying attention in an intentional and purposeful way

- Awareness of the body, mind, and environment

- Nonjudgmental awareness of the present moment

- Grounding oneself with an ethical basis

Mindfulness is not about any of these:

- Having no thoughts

- Bliss

- Relaxation

- Removing all stress

- Avoiding, denying, suppressing, or bypassing afflictive emotions

Mindfulness happens in the now. When we're caught in stories of the past or projections into the future, we're living at least partially in the past or the future. We can be lost in thought and less in touch with what's happening now. Mindfulness practice, such as the breathing practices described at the end of this chapter, helps us return to the present moment, observe what's happening, pause, and choose skillfully from a place of compassionate action rather than reacting out of conditioned habits and patterns.

Real Voices, Real Courage

I met eli tizcareño, a young urban farmer, in 2020, when they and their partner attended a series of virtual retreats for people who identify as Black, Indigenous, and People of Color (BIPOC). By chance, I found myself in a breakout room with eli and their partner and knew I'd lucked out.

When I heard eli speaking powerfully and humbly about their experience as a young trans person, I knew their voice was critical for this book and for understanding soul making, of risking living authentically, to speak up and speak out, and living bravely. Here are eli's words.[8]

eli tizcareño

they/them/elle

MA candidate in urban sustainability, Antioch University; American Friends Service; National Young Farmers Coalition

"The more we practice bravery, the easier it becomes."

I identify as a queer, trans, Mexican American urban educator and farmer, organizer, and facilitator. My parents came from a very small town in Mexico called Ahuisculco, which has precolonial roots in what is now the state of Jalisco, Mexico. In the Nahuatl language, the town's name can be interpreted as "where water serpentines." Indigenous people built homes where water flowed. Over five hundred years ago, the land was violently transitioned into a colonial town that continues to be a conservative religious pueblo today. As someone who spent every summer of my childhood growing up in this pueblo, I feel a heart-connection to this place, yet I also know it's not a place where I can always be; it's a transitory place, a place to visit, to remember, to dream about, and also to be away from in order to care for all of my identities (especially those which are not always welcomed there). On the other side of the unnatural border is the San Fernando Valley on indigenous Fernandeño Tataviam territory, which is where I was born, was raised, and still live today. The valley is where I feel most comfortable.

I'm twenty-nine years old and have been doing political education, community organizing, and urban agriculture work for over ten years. Specifically, I have organized to increase access for green space, food growing, healing-centered spaces for young people of color and Latinx immigrant communities. As I got politicized, this work just became what I did—I realized its potential for healing and inspiring. Doing this work is my own lifelong journey to better understand, stay connected, and learn from those who came before me who had a deep relationship with the ecology around them, including nonhuman life. I do this because I care about those who come after me, and I believe that our generation may not see all the future fruits to come, but each seed we plant matters.

My parents and elders have taught me that there is so much more to life than money. Although stuck in capitalism, I've seen the ways that they have supported each other through the highs and lows of their lives as immigrants in this country. They may have an even stronger heart-connection with the "other side," with their roots in Mexico, even if some of them may never be able to go back safely, due to the immigration system. They teach me that there will be lows and highs, and I must take from life the most of it. I also have young people in my life who have taught me that no dream is too big to dream of and that our work toward a more just world needs to be fun. We are taught as young people that we need to "grow up," but what adults need to do is not let go of that young visionary within them. Adult mentors and young people I've worked with in high school and prison have taught me this is possible to do, and I try my best to honor this part of myself wherever I go. This wisdom from my ancestors, my elders, and young people in my life lives within me, and it guides me when I feel lost, when I feel I do not know enough, when I feel I am alone in this world.

After high school, I was lucky enough to have mentors who taught me that it is okay to be who I am: queer, trans, a Latinx person who speaks Spanglish. My mentors have emboldened me to know I am good, and that has inspired me to be there for others. Growing up, I didn't know how to identify myself, since I didn't have the language or community to understand my gender and racial identity as a young person. This took a toll on me physically, emotionally, and spiritually and manifested in an eating disorder. My body helped me realize something was wrong and guided me to find a supportive community, which led me to a garden and a liberation school, where I learned more about abolition, gender, and queerness for the first time. This led me to gender studies, to community organizing to increase access for growing food, to community, to politicization and advocacy for jobs for young people of color. This liberation school, inspired by the Black-led freedom schools, amplified the lens through which I saw the world, and it led me to come out and continue facilitating similar spaces now a decade later. Learning our histories is powerful medicine to grieve and heal, understand ourselves and each other, make connections, and understand our collective power.

Food and urban farming not only have been my medicine but also have become an organizing tool to build community, learn about systems of power and oppression, envision a future without the state-sanctioned and institutional violence, and take steps toward creating those spaces today. Healing from white supremacy, anti-indigenous and anti-Black racism, is a lifelong process, and I am committed to that process for myself, my community, and those who come after us. As a twenty-nine-year-old, going on thirty, I am learning that I may always hold the pain, and for that reason it is just as important to hold on to joy, laughter, and celebration as we work together.

As an adult, I've realized that bravery is uncomfortable and a growing practice at the same time. The more we practice bravery, the easier it becomes. The more we speak up for ourselves, those we love, and say a loud "yes!" to a dreamy plan or a loud "hell, no!" to a lousy reform, the better we can unapologetically love ourselves and our communities. Today, for me, that means speaking up and not staying silent.

I ask myself, "Who gets harmed when I stay silent?" I'm not here because people stayed silent. I am here because other people pushed against the status quo, against what culture calls "right" when it doesn't feel right in our hearts nor in the experience of our communities, I know I am here because of collective bravery. That fires me up to keep going. My identities and my relationships shaped who I am and how my commitments to justice are intersectional. I am doing this for myself, those I love, and those I do not know. We are connected, and our work must make that connection, no matter where we work or what work we do.

MINDFULNESS PRACTICE: MINDFUL BREATHING

Time Required: 5 minutes or less

Mindful breathing is perhaps the most essential building block of any mindfulness practice and so common we can download apps into our mobile devices to remind us throughout the day to breathe consciously, recognizing what's happening in the present moment. To do this, we need to stop, pause, notice, and breathe, to pivot from autopilot to what is happening here and now, even when what's happening is unpleasant. This mindfulness practice helps restore balance, like pressing the reset button on your computer, so you can proceed refreshed and renewed. It's a mini check-in with yourself, your body, and the moment.

A word of caution: Daily life not only is stressful but also can be traumatizing. For many, practicing mindful awareness of breathing can be emotionally triggering. As I mentioned in the introduction to this book, mindfulness isn't one-size-fits-all. If you're feeling overwhelmed, it's important to remember that mindfulness is not a substitute for appropriate professional medical care.

The following breath practice is designed to help you alleviate stress, bring greater awareness to how you are breathing, and restore calm.

- Come into a comfortable posture either seated, standing, or lying down where you will not be disturbed.

- Allow your spine to be comfortably straight but not rigid, and allow your head, neck, and spine to be aligned.

- Loosen any tight clothing around your waist.

- Allow your eyes to be closed or opened—whatever is comfortable for you.

- Feel your feet on the floor and feel a sense of connectedness and rootedness.

- Place one hand on your belly and the other hand on your chest.

- Observe, without judgment, the rise and fall of your belly.

- Notice the movement of the hand at the belly and the movement of the hand at your chest as you breathe in and out of the nose for ten breath cycles. There is no need to force or control the breath. Just be with the breath as it is.

- Feel the in-breath and feel the out-breath, putting aside judgment.

- Be with the sensations of breathing.

- When you notice that the mind has wandered away from its attention on the breath, gently bring the wandering mind back to the direct bodily sensation of breathing.

- Avoid making yourself into a failure or giving yourself grief; just pivot instead to generate a feeling of being okay and accepting yourself as you are.

- Each time the mind wanders, gently bring the mind back to the sensation of the breath, noticing the in-breath and the out-breath, from the very first sensation of the breath coming into the body to the very last sensation of the breath leaving the body.

- When you're ready, stretch gently and open your eyes if they are closed.

A Short Adaptation

Thich Nhat Hanh taught mindful breathing as a fundamental practice. While there are many forms of this teaching and related practices, I've adapted a simple version for my daily life. You may find this version to be easily memorized and "portable":

Breathing in, I feel my in-breath.
Breathing out, I feel my out-breath.

Following the in-breath, I open.
Following the out-breath, I relax.

Breathing in, I soften.
Breathing out, I let go of worry and tension in my body.

QUERIES

- Where has Spirit, a sense of the Inward Light, been most present for you today?

- How has Spirit, the Inward Light, guided or led you in your work and life now?

- What are you called to be or to do because of this sense of being led by Spirit, the Inward Light?

Chapter 2

DARING TO LISTEN TO THE INNER VOICE, THE SMALL HOLY

Your friend is your needs answered.
He is your field which you sow with love and reap
with thanksgiving.
And he is your board and fireside.
For you come to him with your hunger, and you seek him for peace.
—*Kahlil Gibran*

Close to my home in bucolic Bucks County, Pennsylvania, are many intersecting and walkable country roads. Recently, I walked uphill along Old Carversville Road, following Paunnacussing Creek. Coming to a rustic barn and lumber mill, I was drawn by the glow of light shining through dozens of cracks in the rough-hewn walls. The light through the cracks was diamond-like: light scattered everywhere, illuminating the darkness.

I thought of a dear friend and spiritual mentor, Helen, who had recently passed away from metastatic cancer, and also the many who have died from COVID-19, their light prematurely extinguished. As I write today, hundreds of thousands of people in the United States alone have died from the global pandemic of COVID-19. Helen was a ray of light for me and so many others. She connected me to myself and to the deeper purpose of my life. A Plum Village Dharma teacher, Helen, mentored, nurtured, and supported me. She was a friend who cared about issues of social equity. Even as her physical body was deteriorating from the effects of eight years of cancer treatments, she continued to lead meditation retreats, write articles on spirituality, and mentor countless people, all while seeking to deepen her understanding of race and justice. She wasn't stuck in false optimism or fatal pessimism; instead, she was clear about her values and her intention to be fully alive with her diagnosis. Helen reminded me of the importance of cultivating a curious and open mind and heart. She reminded me that the foundation of mindfulness is tenderness, kindness, and gentleness, which she embodied in her love of life.

In the Gaelic tradition, Helen was an *anam cara*, a soul friend. In the book *Anam Cara*, the great Irish poet and writer

John O'Donohue describes *anam cara* as "a person to whom you could reveal the hidden intimacies of your life."[1] Soul friendships develop slowly, though as Aristotle surmised, the wish for friendship develops quickly. True friendship takes great care and great work, as O'Donohue writes, as with the *anam cara*, you share your "innermost self, your mind and your heart." The *anam cara* is an "act of recognition and belonging," "graced with affection," which is "awakened by friendship." And "when your affection is kindled," continues O'Donohue, "the world of your intellect takes on a new tenderness and compassion." As the shafts of light from the barn illuminated the night, Helen and I shared not just a soul friendship but a sacred connection that awakened me to wild possibilities of moving closer to the meaning of love, the heart of coming in touch with the soul.

Early in our friendship, I expressed my earnest intention to get somewhere with practicing meditation—to grow more insightful, to feel greater peace and clarity, to learn or relearn how to accept and love myself and to do the same with others. I unconsciously made my practice of mindfulness a "project." Just as in my goal-oriented, urgency-driven life, I held myself to impossibly high and unattainable standards, I also held others to that exacting standing. I couldn't see what was happening to me, as though I were looking at a darkened barn from a darkened night. I couldn't see what light might be there. One day Helen asked me, "Are you happy?" Reflexively, I said, "Yes, of course." She asked another question: "What if you gave up trying so hard?"

"What if," she continued, "rather than trying to replace the disappointments, the hurts, the losses in your life with something else, even something far better, you could allow yourself to be softened by them? What if, rather than letting your practice become a project you take on, you allowed everything you have already done to work through you, and trusted that?"

> *A true spiritual partner is one who encourages you to look deep inside yourself for the beauty and love you've been seeking. A true teacher is someone who helps you discover the teacher in yourself.*
>
> *—Thich Nhat Hanh*

I became a lawyer before I knew who I was. I did good work with a sense of satisfaction, yet that came with a hefty price tag: emotionally, relationally, spiritually, and physically, I was drained. While still fully entrenched in a demanding legal career, I started exploring a big life shift. I immersed myself in Buddhism and Quakerism, which led me to enroll in a part-time evening graduate course in holistic spirituality at Chestnut Hill College in Philadelphia. I was leading a kind of double life: by day, I was a lawyer-lobbyist, and at night and on weekends, I was studying theology and practicing Buddhist mindfulness meditation and sitting in meeting for worship with Friends. The tension and push-pull of my day job with my spiritual values felt unresolvable.

During the first few weeks of the semester, I was short-tempered; as the days turned into weeks, my mood grew to boiling-hot mad. It all came to a head one day when a fellow student stopped me just outside a classroom to ask a harmless question, probably directions to a class, and I flew into a rage. After offloading on the student, I apologized. Then I decided to sit down with myself to figure out what exactly was happening with me.

At Chestnut Hill, I was on a collision course between my fragile soul, which was begging for warmth and tenderness, and my full-on, zany drive for success. The truth is that my motive and mindset were shifting in ways I hardly recognized. I went to law school to get out of Brooklyn, to make money, period. I was running fast and furiously from poverty and the trauma of my mother's untimely and devastating death. Impervious to my own inner needs for tenderness and touch, I substituted relentless overdrive in place of being authentic, building connections, and cultivating trust. Studying theology meant I was off the predictable path of a career trajectory with external signals that pointed toward safety: money, a high-status career with a pension and paid leave. Instead, I was following an inward motion, an imperative that I could hardly articulate to myself or understand. I was following the soul. Even today, I continue to fumble for the words to try to explain how I am touched and opened by the soul.

To listen to the voice of the soul, O'Donohue says, is to allow it to be a guide when we forget our deeper nature, our interconnectedness with the world, when we feel unable and desperate to make sense of a world that can be cruel and confusing. "Once the soul awakens," O'Donohue writes, "the search begins, and you can never go back."[2]

Within myself was a tug-of-war pulling between safety and security on one side and the big risk of listening to my soul on the other. I chose a soul-centered life and found new and powerful energy in my studies at Chestnut Hill. Though I attended class after a long workday and long drive, I soaked in the new learning with a sense of homecoming. Ultimately, Chestnut Hill taught me to turn to the personal authority of the soul—its sense of purpose and meaning, a feeling of completeness. The Jungian analyst James Hollis, in his book *Living an Examined Life*, says, "Few of us realize that *it is not what we do but what we are in service to inside that makes the difference*."[3] I made a sharp turn to living in service of the soul: I turned toward an inner willingness and trust, to the tension of life's unfolding in unexpected and unplanned ways. The soul began asking me to dream with questions: What are my gifts? Why was I given this life? What is the soul's desire? These questions are not ones to sidestep or bypass, but instead to see them each as a knock at the door, a wake-up call.

The Soul Voice of the Natural World

> *The door is round and open.*
> *Don't go back to sleep.*
>
> —*Rumi*

The knock on the door of my soul kept getting louder and louder, especially when I walked in the woods or went to a beach, listening to the sound of a bird or seeing a sunset. In those places, I listened to my soul and learned from the senses—most importantly how to slow down. I started a monthly practice called "beach days." This is time set aside to be in nature for a full day or as close as I can to a full day to slow down and practice mindful walking, mindful eating, and mindful breathing. Beach days—what some might call Sabbath days—are a reminder for me to stop, not because I don't have something seemingly important to do, but because stopping and pausing are the right things to do.

Because I am conditioned to keeping going, heeding the nudge to stop is challenging. The part of me that gets momentary satisfaction in crossing off the compelling tasks and projects on the never-ending to-do lists registers protest in the form of anxiety and worry at the very thought of taking a day off from the productivity grind. This is a good place for braving my way toward simplicity and awakening. It's a place where I can face the false impulse that says not doing is unproductive and face my conditioning to drive myself relentlessly forward. And it's a place to choose braver options, such as being unafraid to make myself uncomfortable, to lay down my fears and anxiety, to show up to myself in a larger, unscripted way.

Even with the inner sense that I need to slow down, the experience of fear and discomfort about giving myself a break keeps me going. When I was a couple of months into this practice of intentionally setting aside one day each month to rest and renew, I decided to take the two-and-a-half-hour drive north of New York City to Blue Cliff Monastery, founded by Thich Nhat Hanh, for their weekly Day of Mindfulness. This is a time when mindfulness practitioners gather to learn or relearn the art of living mindfully. After I pulled my Subaru hatchback onto the gravel drive in the early-morning fog, I made my way to the tearoom for a steamy cup of herbal tea. Just being in the monastery, I could feel the muscles in my back ease as I wrapped my hands around a cup of mint tea, the scent a reminder of the rich soil of the monastery's garden.

The day began with sitting meditation, and then an inspiring talk given by one of the monks. I could sense the spreading warmth of calm just being there in the quiet as our group of about thirty people began outdoor walking with mindful awareness in the monastery's pine forest. Stepping over branches and leaf-covered rocks, we came to a greenest-green mossy path, aglow and cushiony-soft, and turned silently toward a rushing stream bursting with patches of whitewater from the early spring rain runoff. We stopped to listen to tumbling waters and take in the scene.

As I stood there, I was overcome with a sense of the perfect order of the forest: the branches crisscrossing each other, the way the water fell downhill over the rocks, a leaf held by wind. I knew intuitively this was a small holy—and the voice of the soul. I was listening and finding another way of knowing, guided by the moment.

* * *

In his book *The Journey of Soul Initiation*, wilderness guide and eco-depth psychologist Bill Plotkin speaks to the Four Windows of Knowing: feeling, imagination, sensing, and thinking.[4] He says these four human faculties are required to understand and appreciate ourselves and the world around us. Plotkin goes on to explain the power and potential of each.

Feeling. Full-bodied feeling includes awareness of emotions, awareness of bodily sensations—internally of bodily organs (interoception) and external limbs (proprioception). This faculty includes intuitive awareness, like "gut feelings" and hunches. Plotkin explains that this full-bodied feeling is essential to form relationships with others and with the natural world.

Imagination. Deep imagination includes dreams and visions that we don't control but that arise "unbidden" and bear the mark of truth. This is the "primary resource for recognizing our emerging future, for 'seeing' the visionary possibilities of what we can create right now—individually and collectively—and consequently for creating a better world."

Sensing. The third faculty is sensing, learning to "reside in the five senses of vision, hearing, taste, smell, and touch." As contemporary people, we're too often far removed from the natural world. In the time of pandemic, many lost their sense of smell, many longed for the touch of another caring human being. This faculty, like the others, requires cultivation.

Thinking. The fourth faculty is heart-centered thinking, which "is not logical, analytical, deductive" but instead is a kind of thinking that is "critical, creative, moral, and compassionate," which "reflectively questions assumptions, discerns hidden values, and considers the larger social and ecological context."

This way of thinking "overflows with animated curiosity," leading us toward change.

* * *

The soul seems to speak loudest through nature, and I am listening. Far from being unproductive, my beach days are a time to take notice of the small holiness of ordinary moments: catching a glimpse of the new moon, hearing the unexpected song of a chickadee, and spending spacious time with friends. Now outside my window, Canada geese fly overhead, calling, calling. This is the time to listen, so I listen.

A NOTICING PRACTICE

This noticing practice comes from my friends at Shao Shan Temple in East Calais, Vermont.

- Notice when you feel the need to explain or defend, particularly when criticized or blamed.

- Notice any body sensations.

- Become aware of your thoughts.

- Experiment with pausing.

- Take a breath and a long slow sigh, and then try that twice more.

- Notice any shift of energy in your body.
- Notice any change in your mindset.
- Make an effort to genuinely listen and consider what the other person is saying, even if you disagree.
- Notice what happens.

Listening seems intuitive, something I should know how to do instinctively. Yet to listen to the language of nature, to another person, to listen to the soul voice, is hard to do. Partly through conditioning, I still am overcommitted, overextended, and distracted. Instead of listening for understanding, I'm preparing a response or rebuttal, filtering what I'm hearing through my own personal lens of conscious and unconscious biases, perceptions, assumptions, values, beliefs, patterns, and more.

Beyond words that are spoken, true listening is not only about what is spoken with words but also about the unsaid. This way of listening engages more than the ears. It is a full-bodied experience of listening with presence, with the eyes to see, the heart to feel, the mind to reflect and discern, with the intuition, an inner knowing that allows for soul connection.

As a lawyer, I was trained to put my emotions aside and focus on "just the facts." I believed that focusing on emotions could open an emotional floodgate I was unprepared to deal with my own rage, grief, and anger. As the big-shot lawyer, I had the answer before the question was asked. In jumping to the answer, I killed connection and relationship—something that brought my shaky and brief first marriage to an end. I murdered understanding with a quick and ready response. Often my husband would say, "You just don't listen to me." And he was right. Strangely, and I don't recommend it, the divorce offered me an opportunity to listen differently. The first thing I did after the divorce was take a course on active listening, learning how to listen from the heart. Far from being touchy-feely, listening for understanding is hard work. And it's worth it.

In my training as an executive coach at Georgetown's Leadership Coaching Program at the Institute for Transformational Leadership and as a facilitator with the Center for Courage & Renewal, cofounded by Parker J. Palmer, I learned listening skills through the Quaker practice of the clearness committee, a process of individual spiritual discernment with others. Listening, I learned, is a creative and interior process that's reciprocal, a giving and receiving. As the listener, I give myself, my attention, and my heart through a presence that is felt beyond the words, and I receive the speaker's presence, words, and energy. It's a reciprocal exchange, a two-way street of taking in and giving out: taking in the words and the nonverbal cues—tone of voice, body gestures, hand and eye movements, and more—and holding them with openness and curiosity rather than jumping to conclusions, checking out emotionally, or reacting impulsively.

After years of practicing this type of listening, I now know the signs that tell me when I'm listening with my heart and when I'm not. When I'm listening and being listened to, there's a glowing sensation at the center of my chest and throat that says something alive and real is happening. Truth is here.

Interpersonal Mindfulness

It may come as a surprise that mindfulness can be practiced while speaking *and* listening. Interpersonal or relational mindfulness, as it's often called, was developed in the United States largely by Gregory Kramer, founding teacher of the Insight Dialogue Community[5]. Interpersonal Mindfulness is a course based on Gregory Kramer's Insight Dialogue Guidelines. The course was originally developed for graduates of the Mindfulness Based Stress Reduction (MBSR) Program. It is a secular, mainstream presentation of the Insight Dialogue Guidelines, just as MBSR is a secular program with Buddhist underpinnings. Within the Plum Village community, mindful communication is an essential practice to express ourselves fully and authentically; it also supports greater understanding between people. The keys to communicating authentically are speaking honestly and listening fully.

While this practice sounds straightforward, it's actually challenging. When I trained as a Plum Village Dharma teacher, I learned the practice of compassionate listening—to listen with the aim of alleviating another's pain, without interrupting, offering explanations, or corrections. Even if I think that what the other person is saying is partially or completely wrong, when I'm practicing mindful listening, it's not the time to offer correction or advice, because the objective isn't to prove that I'm right and the other person is wrong, but instead to alleviate suffering. This practice requires a lot of mindful awareness in order to notice my own emotions, urges, and impulses, and to breathe mindfully to feel grounded. Many times, I don't have the inner stability to listen with equanimity, and I've come to respect my limits. But when I'm able to listen with equanimity, I'm amazed by the experience—by the power of listening without an agenda, without interrupting, without trying to fix the other person, and with full presence. When this happens, the communication moves from accusation or the hook of the story to connecting genuinely, without defensiveness.

Communicating mindfully rests on the Buddhist understanding of Right Speech, which is an element of the Noble Eightfold Path, a guide to transforming suffering within oneself and in the world. Buddhism provides specific guidelines for Right Speech:

- Speak truthfully.

- Don't exaggerate.

- Be consistent.

- Avoid doublespeak (saying one thing to one person and something different to another person about the same subject).

- Use kind, peaceful language.

- Revere life.

Right Speech begins with compassionate listening. At my best, I speak with openness, kindness, truthfulness, and to inspire hope and confidence in myself and the relationship. When I'm in a potentially triggering encounter, especially when there is a possibility of tension and misunderstanding, I return to the training from Plum Village. I find it helpful in making a kind of mental checklist before speaking:

- Is what I am about to say truthful?

- Is what I am about to say useful?

- Is what I am about to say kind?

- Is what I am about to say timely?

- Is this mine to say, or should someone else be speaking?

When I consider these criteria, I often decide it's probably best not to speak or perhaps not to speak in this present moment.

My second marriage ended in slow motion because we really stopped connecting and communicating. We grew apart largely because we couldn't meaningfully speak or listen. Misunderstandings turned to arguments, which led to distance, coldness, distrust, and ultimately separation. Even with all my training as a Dharma teacher, I could not communicate in the loving and mutually respectful way that I wanted with all my heart. Buddhists call this kind of suffering *samyojana*, an internal formation that really binds a person, like a tight knot.

After we separated and then divorced, I doubled down on my commitment to learn how to truly listen and understand my own human shortcomings that contributed to the distance and divorce. As a way to heal myself, I began studying interpersonal mindfulness with the Insight Dialogue Community. There I was supported in engaging six steps in interpersonal mindfulness that helped move me toward healing: pause, relax, open, attune and trust whatever is emerging in the relationship, listen deeply, and speak truthfully. In the following descriptions of these steps, I provide a sample practice for each.

Pause

Pausing allows for awareness of what is happening within us—thoughts, emotions, urges, and more—and what is happening externally in our environment. *Pause* is powerful because we are so conditioned by the strong pull into our heads and out of our bodies. *Pause* is an act of empowerment in a world driven, bullied into doing.

To practice the pause, recall the acronym STOP: stop, take a breath, observe, proceed. Step out of habit and autopilot.

Relax

Relax is making use of the pause to settle and soothe the nervous system, to release built-up tension. We cannot will ourselves to relax. And you can't relax fast. Relaxation happens in layers, like peeling back an onion. It's like taking a warm bath or sinking into a feather bed. We meet whatever is happening with kindness, a softening. *Relax* is not about sleepiness but instead is a feeling of tranquility and equanimity.

While I know this to be true, relaxing is still hard for me to do. Even as I wake up in the morning before I get out of bed, there's the urge to get going, to get a jump on things. I have to intentionally catch myself and, even as I lie in bed, practice slowing down: stretching, breathing, taking my time, feeling a tiny bit of gratitude for this moment. This practice sets a tone for my day, beginning before I even get out of bed in the morning. The statement I'm making these days is "I don't have to rush. There's time. I have choice. I can rest a bit." This tamps down the well-practiced sense that everything is urgent. It offers me a moment of space.

Open

To *open* is to bring awareness to the present moment without becoming entangled, without embellishment, meaning without making a story about what's happening: *She said this. He said that. It's never going to work out for me.*

The discipline is to notice when we are carried away by story or, more elusively, using story to dodge painful, buried, or unexamined emotions or more. Being open is like watching a swinging door: the door opens and closes. It's like watching the ocean: the tide comes in and goes out. It's like the sound of wind bells: ting, ting, ting; sound comes and goes. To practice *open* is to notice without grasping, attaching, or entangling, which puts us at the edge of not knowing, uncertainty, and ambiguity. To practice *open* is to practice "beginner's mind," a mind that is curious and flexible. It helps to practice this in small steps, to notice whether I can stay even a tiny bit more open than I did in the past, breaking this down into small, digestible moments of noticing when I am less-rigidly clinging to my ideas of right or wrong.

This was the hardest step for me. I had spent a couple of decades as a lawyer trying hard to be the smartest person in the room, carefully measuring success in what I could prove, buy, or own. My life was the opposite of openness. Instead, I was a grabbing onto life out of scarcity and distrust. What actually began to open me was heartbreak, over and over again. After my second divorce, I realized yet again that allowing the broken openness had a purpose. It shape-shifted me into a different, less cynical, more forgiving version of myself.

Attune to Emergence

To *attune to emergence* is to let go of our agenda and receive things as they are. This doesn't mean we don't have preferences; it means for the time being, we can notice our preference and let them go, meeting the moment as it is. There is an element of trust, surprise, and receptivity. Again, this can be done in small movements, such as suspending judgment to really listen.

This guideline has helped me remember that something is always in the process of emerging. Sometimes what emerges is a shaky sense of trust, sometimes it is a feeling of not getting the other person or them not getting me, sometimes it's speaking a need. Trusting whatever emerges opens the way for acceptance and understanding, for living a more hope-filled life. We can say something like "I'm okay with what's happening now. I trust what's happening between us."

Listen Deeply

Far too often, we listen to react or for confirmation or to evaluate, formulating the response in our heads as the speaker is speaking. We are judging, assessing, critiquing, even as the speaker is speaking. Our listening can be tinged with an edge of wanting to be right. From neuroscience, we know our thinking tends toward the negative—the so-called negativity bias, which means it's easy for us to see what's wrong and harder to see what's right.

This habitual pattern can be changed. A truism in neuroscience is "Neurons that fire together wire together." The brain has plasticity. It's malleable and can change throughout the life span. That means we can unlearn poor listening skills and retrain the brain. Through practice, we can shift passing states, like gratitude, appreciation, and acceptance, into lasting traits. *Listen deeply* is about noticing these hardwired patterns and then making choices that support greater connection, greater understanding.

Speak Truthfully

As with the Buddhist practice of Right Speech, *speak truthfully* in the Insight Dialogue Community is about speaking with honesty and kindness. To speak truthfully is to bring together all the elements of interpersonal mindfulness: pause, relax, open, attune to emergence, and listen deeply. Speaking truthfully also requires another related element: courage grounded in compassion and care. Recently, I made the choice to speak truthfully with a friend. I was feeling down as the days were growing darker and fall was turning quickly to winter. I shared my feelings meaningfully and vulnerably, and I was met with a new level of understanding in the friendship.

SEVEN FACTORS OF AWAKENING: THE SECOND FACTOR, INVESTIGATION

Building on the first factor, mindfulness, *investigation* is about learning from experience to choose wisely, to understand, discern, and distinguish what is a healthy state of mind and what is not. Investigation invites us to ask ourselves what is working and what is not and then adjust accordingly. It's about appreciating clarity and confusion and cultivating genuine, open-ended inquiry. To investigate is to let go of resolution for the moment to appreciate the vitality of the unknown. We become radical learners, resisting the urge to reduce inquiry to fixed and ready-made answers. Investigation tests the limits of what you know while holding this with curiosity and openness.

Real Voices, Real Courage

When I think of a gifted communicator, LoAn Nguyen comes to mind. She is a joyful person, and I was immediately drawn to her smile, the clarity of her words, and the suffering she endured in immigrating to the United States from Vietnam. She shares a bit of this story and how she transformed her beliefs to support her trans daughter, listening to the inner voice, the small holy.

LoAn Nguyen

she/her/hers/cô

LGBTQIA+ advocate, immigrant, war refugee, supporter of a trans child

> *"Bravery means being willing to move out of the norm to show support."*

I was child number seven out of eight that my parents had who survived. I was born in 1963 in Saigon, and my father was in a very high-ranking position with the government. In fact, he was the mayor of Danang for two terms. He was a colonel in the army, working with a White House attaché, so he had a lot of privilege and power in his role. I knew him to be a kind person. My mother never had to work professionally because she married my father. She became like a matron, moving from city to city and managing a brood of children. She was very resourceful as a woman, as a wife, and as a mother, even though each of us got a wet nurse or nanny. We lived in an extended family where relatives from the village came up and helped out. That seems to be the culture of earlier days in Vietnam.

We went to a Catholic convent school because our ancestry was devout Catholic even in this small village, north of Hội An, a village called Quang Tri. It's right on the border between North and South Vietnam. That's our village, where our family ancestry is very strong in the Catholic faith—lots of families, lots of children, lots of faith. My oldest brother is like a prince. In Vietnamese culture, boys have twice the value of girls. I say that because I experience that. I am at the tail end of a string of six girls.

My mother had one older son and then a string of six girls. I am girl number six, and then my younger brother was born. I've always had this sense of injustice as I was growing up: feeling unwanted and like I didn't belong. I was the last girl child that was born before the boy child, so I always had this sense that "oh, that's not fair." But this is what life was all about then.

I developed observation skills early on. My sisters and brothers were sent to convent schools and sent to private music lessons and were given a beautiful piano to practice at home. I thought, "Oh, good! One day, I'll go there too!" But I never got there, because the country fell apart and we were taken out of Vietnam as refugees.

My father had gotten an early retirement from the army and took the entire family of eight kids to the southern tip of Vietnam, called Phu Quoc Island. He had bought passage for all of us. He was such a patriotic nationalist that he would not leave himself unless something forced him to. As we waited for the ship to come to pick us up, every day my mom and older siblings would listen to the news of the country to hear news of our father. And then all of us kids would go to the beach. One day, we were told to come home. We were in our bathing suits. We threw on a pair of shorts and were ushered to the shore. By then, the entire island of people was down by the shore, waiting for the ship that my mom and dad had purchased passage for us on. But the ship couldn't come in because there were so many people that it could not pick up everybody.

My father saw a barge leaving, and he went to the navy general and flashed his badge. The navy general said, "Okay, your family can come on my ship." My father ushered us to a side corner, and I remember we were all running into this barge, and we were picked up and thrown into the barge quickly because masses of people were running after us, also wanting to get on the boat. It was a dire situation. I remember looking behind me, and I saw this elderly woman pulling a big bag and I ran back to help her. My family was already on the barge, and they were yelling at me, "What are you doing? Turn around! Come back!" and I remember being picked up and tossed into the barge just before it left. There were Vietnamese people on the docks who had no way to get out on the water, so I felt an immense sense of just being taken away.

I feel that the experience of being born as girl number six really colored my world perspective. I was someone who understood what it meant to not be chosen, so seeing this older woman wanting to be on this barge, I thought, "I'm going to go help you. Let's do it together," and I went back to help her.

On the barge the navy general let my family get on. We got out to sea and onto a Vietnamese Coast Guard ship. We stayed on that ship for a couple of nights. At nighttime, all the lights had to be turned off because you could hear North Vietnamese planes flying overhead. We could be shot. And people were coming to the barge in whatever floating devices they found, asking to be rescued. Some sailors who wanted to get home traded places with the boat people. Soldiers climbed down as the boat people climbed up. People were shouting, money was being thrown. It was a chaotic moment of leaving and coming and people crying. It was amazing to think I was able to witness that.

A few nights out, another smaller Vietnamese Coast Guard ship came along, and my father made the decision to take our family onto that smaller vessel. That's how we eventually made our way to the Philippine Islands. When we arrived on the island of Subic Bay, we stood in line for food and were living in tents in an American compound, waiting to go to America. Everybody wanted to go to California because its climate was similar to Vietnam's. My dad said, "No, we're not going there, because the wait is too long." When a camp opened up at Fort Chaffee in Arkansas, our family flew to Arkansas in an American plane.

I remember going into the white wooden barracks there at Fort Chaffee in Arkansas. There was a horse outside, and I thought, "What a strange world!" Now we were official refugees. We would again get in line to get food. My dad said our family was too big to be supported by one sponsor, so we needed to split up. The four youngest children went with my parents to Arvada, Colorado, because there was a Baptist family who sponsored us there. That was the beginning of us being resettled into American culture. But within a year and a half, my dad had moved us to California, where the rest of the family joined us. All of a sudden, we had a four-bedroom with ten people in it.

My mom and dad worked at a Subway sandwich shop. They worked as assemblers, as security guards for an insurance company, as teacher's aides, taking on many different jobs so that all of us could go to school. That was the beginning of our life in America.

We all made it out of Vietnam intact. My mother and father continued to remind us how blessed we were as a family. None of us had lost our lives; we were all together. I truly believe that their faith, their prayers, their good karma kept us together. My father is the only one in my entire family that has passed away so far—five or six years ago. Other than that, all of us are intact. We all graduated from colleges, all are working professionals or have children and families of our own. We are so blessed.

Each one of us grew up in a different environment, but we all grew up westernized. I think I'm the most westernized because I was one of the youngest. I was the first one in the family to go to graduation night and prom and all the things high school graduates liked to do. I dove into the mainstream culture and became successful in school. I thought, "Oh, this is my opportunity! I can be someone. I don't have to be the youngest girl."

That feeling of not being wanted and not belonging, that feeling I had in the past, has shifted. The more I give it air and talk about it, the more I'm sensing that it has shifted. That was a gift for me to have gained that sense of empathy so young, and I no longer fault my mother or my family. I actually think it was a gift that shaped my life to be brave and courageous and comfortable with the pain of not being part of something. I really think that is what shaped me.

I think that bravery means being with discomfort—having the fortitude to be on my own and following my gut instinct when others around me are critical of my choices. That's what it means to me. And it means being all right with not belonging until my people and my tribe show up. Bravery means being kind to others when they are not part of the majority. Bravery means being willing to move out of the norm to show support.

One of the most defining moments of my life was to be there and say to my trans kid, "Oh, honey, I don't know what this means, but we'll move through this together." Choosing to love and choosing to be a shield for my child—that was my decision. I learned as much as I could about what it means to be transgender.

In my family, I am different. Accepting the differences means I can allow the opinions of others without fear of conformity, without fear of having to play a role in life or within the family. I think there is something about a willingness to let things be and feeling liberated from constraints. I've come up with a recent mantra that is really resonating with me, and that is "Don't obstruct karma." Get out of the way. Don't obstruct karma. Let things be where they need to be. That is an act of bravery.

MINDFULNESS PRACTICE: DEEP LISTENING

Time Required: 15 minutes
Participants: 2

Elaine Retholtz, a meditation teacher I studied with at New York Insight Center, offers a powerful practice of interpersonal mindfulness. I've incorporated her teaching with that of the Plum Village community to offer this practice of deep listening between two people.

- Set aside technology.

- Acknowledge yourself and your intention to practice meditation, offering yourself a moment of kindness and appreciation, a kind of pat on the back for making the choice to pause and practice.

- Set a clear intention for practicing interpersonal mindfulness. Ask what would be most meaningful. We know how easy it is to read or think *about* mindfulness; it's much harder to have the direct experience of practice.

- Notice pleasant, unpleasant, and neutral sensations. Simply allow them to be and let go.

- Practice *pause*. Become aware of your breathing, sensations, or environment. Feel the ground beneath you. Notice the sense of being supported without needing to run, rush, or do anything in particular.

- *Relax* the body as best you can and notice what happens. Face your partner with your eyes open and without distractions. Preparing to listen in this way could take a few minutes and sets the foundation for real connecting and understanding.

- Here's a prompt to practice in this interpersonal space: *What change is occurring in your life now? What does it feel like in the heart and mind?*

- Notice the pull to be drawn into the words of a story. Instead, stay with the feelings, sensations, and emotions.

- Agree on the order of speaker, where both speaker and listener use the Insight Dialogue Community's guidelines for interpersonal mindfulness, noted earlier in this chapter: *pause, relax, open, attune to emergence, listen deeply,* and *speak truthfully.*

- Agree on the structure for the time. Speaker A speaks for five minutes without interruption as Speaker B practices listening deeply. Pause and then switch. Now Speaker A becomes the listener, and Speaker B shifts from listener to speaker. Speaker B speaks for five minutes to the same prompt, and then both have an open dialogue for five minutes about what both notice.

QUERIES

- How might listening to your inner voice, the small holy, support you and your relationships?

- What challenges in your daily life interrupt your capacity to listen to the inner voice, the small holy?

- What is the risk in listening and then acting on this inner voice, the small holy?

Chapter 3

WHEN LIFE BREAKS YOU OPEN: PRACTICE AND GROWTH

There is a brokenness
out of which comes the unbroken.

—*Rashani*

I was drawn to Buddhism because of its clear path of practice and healing. I loved the silence and simplicity of sitting, walking, and eating meditation. Because suffering seemed to follow me, I wanted to understand the Buddhist teachings on the nature of suffering, the Four Noble Truths. Though simple, maybe even obvious, these statements of truth are profound:

The Four Noble Truths

1. Life contains suffering.
2. Understand the causes of suffering.

3. There is an end to this suffering.
4. There is a path, a way out of suffering.

These teaching are sometimes misunderstood, and some label Buddhism as depressive, a downer, or negative. The teachings do not say that all life is suffering, but instead that life *contains* suffering, which is a continuum from mere disappointment to catastrophe.

When you recognize the universality of suffering, you begin to understand that there are many causes of suffering, most notably our own craving and desire, which are a form of suffering resulting from not accepting things as they are. Of course, it's easy to accept the things you like. It's much harder to accept people and things you don't, and that's the challenge. It's not enough for us to understand what drives suffering or that there is a way out of suffering. Even suffering doesn't last forever; everything changes. What is important for us is to follow the path toward well-being, which is the Buddha's teachings on the Noble Eightfold Path:[1]

The Noble Eightfold Path

1. **Right View.** A true understanding of how reality and suffering are intertwined.
2. **Right Resolve.** The aspiration to act with intention, doing no harm.

3. **Right Speech.** Abstaining from lying and from divisive or abusive speech.

4. **Right Action.** Acting in ways that do not cause harm, such as not taking life, not stealing, and not engaging in sexual misconduct.

5. **Right Livelihood.** Making an ethically sound living, being honest in business dealings.

6. **Right Effort.** Endeavoring to give rise to skillful thoughts, words, and deeds and renouncing unskillful ones.

7. **Right Mindfulness.** Being mindful of one's body, feelings, mind, and mental qualities.

8. **Right Concentration.** Practicing skillful meditation informed by all of the preceding seven aspects.

Together, these teachings of the Four Noble Truths and the Noble Eightfold Path helped me understand my suffering and have it be in service of something much bigger than the grief I was experiencing in the moment. In the Plum Village tradition, we're encouraged to engage Buddhism and its teaching through our life experience and not to be caught up in theory or dogma.

I understood suffering and broken-openness yet again when I traveled to Japan on pilgrimage. While there, I fell in love with the art of preparing tea, which feels like slowing down time. To serve and study tea is to study mindful awareness based on Japanese values of harmony, respect, purity, and tranquility. It is a practice of cultivating beauty in small, very ordinary acts: lighting the charcoal burner or brazier, folding the tea napkin, holding the tea tray, pouring the tea, arranging the tea sweets, and more.

When I returned home, by chance, a local Korean woman offered a class in the art of tea, and I was excited to join and begin studying tea. My Korean teacher came from a long ancestral lineage connected to the art of tea. Her mother studied and taught tea for decades, and her family owned a small factory that made teacups by hand. One day I was busy in the kitchen, arranging the napkins and tea sweets on a tray. My teacher asked me to get one of her family's precious heirloom cups from the cabinet and place it on the tea tray. I walked slowly and handled the earthen cup with great care. Just then, somehow my hands slipped from around the cup, and it fell to the ground and shattered into many pieces. It all happened in slow motion. *Crash!*

I felt a lump in my throat and a knot in my chest as I looked at the cup smashed into pieces. I apologized over and over again and offered to pay for the cup. My teacher turned to me, smiled, and said, "Now the cup is worth even more. It can be transformed by *kintsugi.*" *Kintsugi,* she explained, is the Japanese method of repairing broken ceramics with lacquer dusted with powdered gold. It treats breakage and repair as part of the history of an object, rather than something to disguise; it draws attention to the object's imperfections as a way to make it whole, giving the flaws a focal point of the piece.

This practice, though particular to the Japanese, is also found in other cultures, including the Diné (Navajo) of the southwest United States. While studying weaving with a master weaver at Ghost Ranch, I learned that the Diné deliberately weave an imperfection into a corner of their textiles. It's said that is "where the Spirit moves in and out." Among the Diné, weavers entwine a part of themselves into the textile. There is a single line of contrasting color extending from the center to the edge of the textile, the spirit line or spirit pathway. The spirit line allows the trapped part of the weaver's spirit to exit safely, separating the weaver from any harmful thoughts that they may come in contact with as the textile is used, sold, or exhibited. Among the Diné, the so-called imperfect has an important role. In Japan, the "imperfection" makes the cup more valuable.

"A heart that has been consistently exercised through conscious engagement with suffering is more likely to break open instead of apart," writes Parker Palmer. "Such a heart has learned how to flex to hold tension in a way that expands its capacity for both suffering and joy."[2] The heart of brokenness is not a weakness, says researcher Brené Brown about vulnerability, something she sees as our essential work. "The uncertainty, risk, and emotional exposure we face every day are not optional. Our only choice is a question of engagement. Our willingness to own and engage with our vulnerability determines the depth of our courage and the clarity of our purpose; the level to which we protect ourselves from being vulnerable is a measure of our fear and disconnection."[3]

The Four Noble Truths and the Noble Eightfold Path are about engaging life and suffering without turning away from what breaks you, and instead leaning in wholeheartedly. What breaks your heart reminds you of what you love and what you live for. At times, my heart breaks explosively in shards of sadness. Rather than deny, suppress, or ignore that sadness, I accept myself, the vulnerability, the brokenness, the "gold" that repairs the soul. My heart breaks, and it is softer and more supple because of suffering.

The Art of Suffering

In 2014, Thich Nhat Hanh offered a worldwide tour titled "The Art of Suffering." Thousands of people joined the retreat to learn how to skillfully address their suffering. Nhat Hanh has written more than a hundred books and given countless Dharma talks on the topic of suffering and mindfulness, and they all contain a similar message: the energy and practice of mindfulness, concentration, and insight help us to embrace suffering and to calm the body and mind to be peace and create peace in the world, to be love and to create love.

You might be thinking, "What does suffering have to do with love?" This is often answered by anyone who has lost a loved one: grief is there because love is there. This is something I realized yet again when my brother Trevor passed away in 2020. Everybody leaves something behind when they die. Trevor left behind countless moments of love, including the holidays squeezed into his Upper West Side apartment, the dining room table laden with dishes he loved to cook. He left behind a love of orchids growing on the windowsill in the bright sunlight. He left behind days and weeks spent in his beloved second home in Jamaica, puttering around the garden for endless hours in the day. It's true the grief of his death is there. Yet grief is there because of these moments of love.

In four words, Thich Nhat Hanh summed up the art of suffering: "No mud, no lotus." Happiness and suffering are interconnected. You cannot grow a lotus flower without mud. Life breaks you open to both pain and potential.

Members of the Plum Village community take a vow to help others understand and transform their suffering, the brokenness that is integral in living. Many people I encounter as potential coachees, retreatants, and pilgrims believe that they need certain internal or external conditions to feel okay, to feel happiness or joy. They think if they get rid of their anger, fear, self-doubt, and rage, they can replace it with something that will feel better, or if they get the right partner, the right job, the right car, they'll be happy. In the Plum Village community, our practice is to take very good care of these afflictive emotions like sadness, grief, and resentment in the same way we care for our compassion, patience, and love. This is the art of suffering well. We learn how to handle suffering, knowing that it is the basis for our happiness.

> *I do not believe that sheer suffering teaches. If suffering alone taught, the world would be wise, since everyone suffers. To suffering must be added mourning, understanding, patience, love, openness, and the willingness to remain vulnerable.*
>
> —Anne Morrow Lindbergh

SEVEN FACTORS OF AWAKENING: THE THIRD FACTOR, ENERGY

The Third Factor of Awakening is energy, which means effort, to apply oneself to the task, to be attentive to details, to be concentrated. It's like a focused beam of light illuminating a dark room that keeps us on track, not wasting time or energy with the trivial. Implicit in this way of being is self-respect and self-discipline to make choices that truly support and nourish you, not only in the present moment but also as you create meaning and purpose in your life. The following well-known Zen poem, a poignant verse that is often recited in the evening at the close of the day, is a reminder of the brevity of life and the importance of applying our life energies skillfully:

> Let me respectfully remind you:
> Life and death are of supreme importance.
> Time passes swiftly by and opportunity is lost.
> Let us awaken, awaken. Take heed.
> Do not squander your life.

Real Voices, Real Courage

American Quaker, author, and activist George Lakey is a prominent member of the Religious Society of Friends. I have known George for many years and have long admired his work for social justice and peace, his plainspoken honesty and truth telling. In my leadership work, I've relied on his book Facilitating Group Learning: Strategies for Success with Diverse Adult Learners. *My copy is filled with Post-it Notes and highlighting, and virtually every page is loaded with wisdom that comes from his hard-earned experience. Reading his narrative, I see a connection with "No mud, no lotus," as George has faced life-threatening challenges in* pursuit of courageous values of justice and peacemaking. He has made good use of suffering in service of a better world. My conversation with George begins with—of all things—a charming personal story about meeting a Quaker lion tamer.

George Lakey

He/him

Quaker activist and sociologist

"Bravery is about caring. When I think of instances when I have acted with courage, with bravery, I really cared about the outcome and understood being brave would make the difference."

I have several stories about how I learned bravery. I was on a Quaker-sponsored Spanish-speaking tour in Europe. I was picked up in a local town in Holland, by a man who was a hospitality practitioner. While driving me back, he told me that most of his career had been as a lion tamer. I said, "Whoa, that sounds fantastic! Tell me more. I've never met a lion tamer and certainly not in Quaker circles. So what's that like?"

He began telling me, and when we got to his home, he said, "Well, we're home now. Now I can show you my scrapbook." So I'm paging through his scrapbook, and one of the big pictures shows him with his head in the jaws of the lion—the classic photo. And I say, "Man, you are the bravest person I've ever met in my life. How could that be?"

He said, "I'm strange. Most lion tamers are very brave because they're very scared of the possible consequences and making mistakes, but as a small boy, I happened to have fallen in love with cats—tabbies, domestic pussycats. As I grew older and got acquainted with larger cats, I still saw them as pussycats and loved them. It was natural for me to take up a career as a lion tamer, and I just always saw them as my kitties. They saw me act that way toward them, so I had an affectionate relationship with the cats."

"I never used the whip on them," he said, "and we developed a relationship such that I could be nonviolent with them. They understood me, and I understood them. Once I made a mistake and was in the hospital, but not for very long."

So he had this great relationship with lions, tigers, and even bears. He said, "Where that leaves me is that I have to find other ways of being brave."

"What do you mean?" I asked. He said, "Bravery is about doing something when you're scared. Because I didn't happen to be scared in my line of work, I now have had to find other ways of acting in response to my fear in other parts of my life and acting in spite of it. That's what courage is."

Listening to him was a new way for me to look at courage and see that it's the opportunity to see what you're afraid of doing and then doing it anyway.

Over and over, I've been in situations that scared me. The fact that I'm upwardly mobile and was brought up in a blue-collar family—I've tried to hobnob with professional middle-class people, especially people with a stamp on their forehead of being the high-end, noble, aristocratic types. That is always scary for me. I'm never comfortable with them, with the exception of my lover. I actually made friends at one point in my life with a guy from a wealthy family. It took him a year of friendship to come out to me, even as I had come out to him much earlier. He was an activist who wore thrift store clothes. When he came out to me, I said, "Why have you been so slow about this?" And he said, "Because I was afraid you'd dump me, since I know how strongly you identify with the working class. You see the rich as oppressing you, so I was afraid you'd walk out on me." He said this even as we actually shared the same politics.

There have been exceptions, but for the most part, I'm really out of my comfort zone a lot of the time. At several points in my life, a knife has been pulled on me. Once I stepped between somebody with a gun and a person he wanted to kill. I've been in a number of objectively dangerous situations where I realize, "Uh-oh, this is dangerous," and do it anyway. Very often in my life, I've felt fear for objective reasons—there was an actual threat—and I was brave in those situations in the sense that I acted rationally, calmly, and in a way that kept me alive and also resolved the situation.

My mother and dad were great examples for me because they emphasized that what matters most is what you end up doing. In our family, family comes first; we come through for each other. So whatever we have to handle, we do it in order to be able to come through.

When I was just a boy, my parents taught me that performance matters. It's about getting it done, whatever the task is, however scary it might be. I got into public speaking in eleventh grade. I was challenged to do that by my English teacher, and I noticed that every single time I got up to make a speech, I felt nervous. I had stage fright over and over and over, but I did it because I was challenged to do it. It was also satisfying to actually come through for myself—to do what I said I would do—and I kept experiencing rewards for handling the fear in a way that didn't prevent me from coming through.

Both the parental example and then getting challenged along the way to handle my fear to be able to do what I wanted to do set me on a lifelong expectation that a lot of things you do in your life will be hard, they will be scary, and you'll do them anyway. So meeting the Quaker lion tamer was really helpful, because he was also saying, "Hey, it's a plus to be brave."

A lot of us aspire to put courage on our list of virtues. We think, "Well, we're expanded as human beings when we act courageously. We're bigger when we're courageous." So that's why this lion tamer had to find other ways of being brave, because he reached toward that virtue. That conversation with him was really helpful in that it affirmed what I'd already intuitively guessed.

Bravery is about caring. When I think of instances when I have acted with courage, with bravery, I really cared about the outcome and understood being brave would make the difference, would make some consequential difference where bravery wasn't frivolous at all. Bravery could go either way in terms of the results. But it seemed that I cared deeply about the situation where I brought necessary bravery.

When I think of the Quaker lion tamer, he would say bravery is when you do what you need to do, despite being scared to do it. So being brave is the handling of the fear. I won't say "overcoming" the fear. I never got the Gandhi piece when I faced fear. Gandhi used to intentionally lead people into scary, life-threatening situations. The British police would shoot you. It was the racism thing, right? Gandhi kept saying to his people, "Become fearless," and that never sat right with me. I fell in love with Gandhi in graduate school. I read everything I could about him, and I fell in love with his vision for nonviolence in general, but I thought, "I have a bone to pick with you there. I don't agree that we need to be fearless." What I am okay with is fearing and doing anyway. And maybe that is the way that a Hindu talks about fearlessness as culturally and religiously appropriate. But anyway, I knew that my goal would not be fearlessness.

Here's another surprising angle on this topic. It involves my son-in-law, who is a concert pianist. I talked with him about stage fright because the stakes were high for his performances, and half the audience already knows the classical music piece, so they know if he makes a mistake. They've heard the concerto before, so the expectations are very high. "What's that like for you?" I asked him. "How do you handle that?"

"We are taught in conservatory that we have a button we can press," he said. "When that fear comes and we press the button, we turn it into excitement." So we read it differently. When our heart is beating faster and the adrenaline is flowing, we read that physiological response of the body as excitement and say, "Oh, good. I'm excited that I'll play this Chopin concerto." He said, "They teach us that trick systematically in conservatory: 'Oh, good! My heart's beating faster? Hey, I'm excited about this!' By redefining the situation, we support ourselves to a splendid performance."

MINDFULNESS PRACTICE: HANDLING STRONG EMOTIONS

Time Required: 5 minutes or less

Sometimes you're filled with strong emotions that feel like too much to handle or you feel broken open by life. The Plum Village tradition trains us in practices that help us turn mud into lotus flowers. It begins with the breath. First, I was trained to bring my breathing and my awareness down into my abdomen, to feel the rise and fall of my belly and my breath. Then I learned to visualize myself rooted like a tree or solid as a mountain. This visual image, combined with the practice of breathing deep and low into the belly, helps a person regain stability and calm.

Here are some steps to practice at those moments of feeling intense emotion:

- When you feel broken open by life, stop, pause, and breathe.

- Become aware of your feet on the ground, your roots.

- Connect with a sense of internal groundedness and stability.

- Bring your awareness to your breathing, especially to the area below the navel.

- Breathe deeply, focusing on this place in the body.

- Visualize an image to support your breathing: a mountain, a large, rooted oak tree, or something else that speaks to a sense of stability.

- Continue for a few breaths.

- When you are ready, stretch.

QUERIES

Describe a time when you felt broken open. Bring these queries to your reflection on that time:

- How is holding your own brokenness helpful to your healing?

- How might your feeling of brokenness be in service of something larger than yourself?

- How would holding your brokenness support you in strengthening compassion, both for yourself and for others?

Chapter 4

TRUSTING TRUE SELF: TAKING THE RISK TO BLOSSOM

And the day came when the risk to remain tight in a bud was more painful than the risk it took to blossom.

—*Anaïs Nin*

It's just past mud season as I write, which means this is an in-between time of year. It's not quite full-blown summer with the abundance of fruits and fresh vegetables, yet early spring flowers have already come and gone. This in-between time, shifting in slow movement, may hardly be noticeable unless you're paying attention. When I lived in the city, I barely noticed this transition, but in my barnlike home outside of Philadelphia, these shifts in nature are evident—or perhaps I am more attuned to them.

Full of hope, I moved here about twelve years ago with strong memories of my soul-sensing time planting garlic at Ghost Ranch. The barn and my tiny plot of land filled me with dreams of growing a flower garden. Now I am here, fully here. I notice the return of spring songbirds outside my windows: spring red-breasted nuthatches, tree swallows, black-capped chickadees, and gray catbirds.

Spring is a time that pushes into new life, inviting us to try something new, seek a fresh start. It was in a late spring more than twenty years ago that I accepted the invitation, when I walked into Riverside Church in Manhattan and listened to the Dharma talk given by Thich Nhat Hanh. That day, which I wrote about earlier, changed my life.

That talk invited me toward deeper understanding. I began to notice, question, and engage my inner life—my thoughts, values, beliefs, and intuition. I began to make the connection between this inner life and cues in my physical body. I began to deeply question whether my values were aligned with my work in the world. My decision to go to law school was largely driven by fear, willpower, and determination—motivations that carried me through most of my career. Despite being overwhelmed in my career, I was determined not to give up. And in my determination to succeed, I began to understand I was losing a vital part of myself.

After attending the Dharma talk at Riverside Church, I began practicing mindfulness with the Plum Village community, joining and then founding a local *sangha*—a Buddhist community sharing the practice of mindfulness meditation. Two nights out of the week, I practiced mindfulness meditation with local groups, and on Sundays, I joined my local Quaker meeting for silent worship.

To make sense of my thoughts, I poured my feelings into journals while I attended retreats and continued a daily meditation practice. This was in sharp contrast to my work life. As a stressed-out lawyer, I worked fourteen-hour days and fell into bed at night exhausted. I went on like this for almost twenty years. I was in an internal fight to keep going on the hamster wheel of work-sleep-eat-work, even as I sought to make space for another part of my life being created from my inner spiritual work.

Since I spent so much time at work, I decided to begin practicing meditation while there. I began with a body scan practice, paying close attention to what was happening within my body, to sensations, as I was working. As a lobbyist, my job focused on persuading politicians often while standing together with them in the halls of the state capitol or the US Congress. I practiced paying attention to my feet on the ground and reflecting on what I was doing and how I was doing it. I mentally scanned my body, from the feet up, noticing sensations in my legs, thighs, hips, stomach, chest, back, shoulders, face, and jaw. I noticed constriction or tightness and the fluttery feeling in my stomach.

Then I would shift my attention from these physical sensations in my body to paying attention to the person—usually a local politician—I was speaking to. I became curious about this person, wanting to understand their perspective rather than doggedly holding to my agenda. As I shifted my attention and interest to the other person, I felt a gentle opening in my heart, which signaled that something was happening within me and in my relationship with the other person. I began to take genuine and sincere interest in each person I spoke with. There was a softening within me, and the need to be right fell away. I could be me. I could listen. I didn't need to persuade or try to change the other person. There was a ground of mutuality and understanding. From within me, a way of being shifted my way of working, my exterior life. People would remark, "Gee, you don't seem like a lawyer." Under my breath, I would respond, "What's the matter with you?" I couldn't see what was becoming obvious to those I lobbied: the steady soul-enlarging spiritual practices I was doing on a daily basis—the journaling, the meditation in community, the body scan, the noticing, the softening—all of it had changed me from the inside out. I was no longer a lawyer-lobbyist. So, who was I becoming?

Vocation is "not a goal to be achieved but a gift to be received," wrote Parker Palmer in his book, *Let Your Life Speak*.[1] In the book, he speaks about the movement toward vocation: "Discovering vocation does not mean scrambling toward some prize just beyond my reach but accepting the treasure of True Self I already possess. Vocation does not come from a voice 'out there' calling me to become something I am not. It comes from a voice 'in here' calling me to be the person I was born to be to fulfill the original selfhood given me at birth by God."

What was happening within those halls of power and influence, in Congress and the state capitol where I lobbied and practiced mindful awareness, was a growing realization, combined with my inner work strengthening the voice "in there," calling me toward myself. And part of that process included fear, anxiety, hesitation, and uncertainty. Even as I wanted one hundred percent certainty, I understood that certainty was at odds with the process of trusting emergence. I was no longer the role I had adopted in life, the role of the lawyer. I was enlarging my life from the inside out toward a vision that was in formation.

"Anxiety is the price of a ticket on the journey of life; no ticket—no journey; no journey—no life," writes James Hollis, the Jungian analyst, in *Swamplands of the Soul: New Life in Dismal Place*.[2] He goes on to say:

We may run from anxiety as much as possible but we thereby run from our only life. . . . Again, we are daily forced to choose between depression and anxiety. Depression results from the wounding of the individuation imperative; anxiety results from moving forward into the unknown. The path of anxiety is necessary because therein lies the hope of the person to more nearly become an individual. . . . Courage is not the absence of fear. It is the perception that some things are more important to us than what we fear.

I was choosing courage, hope. Even though emotionally I was torn between wanting safety and security, everything I worked so hard to achieve, the soul voice called me like a homing device forward toward the unknown with no guarantees, no promises other than this guiding feeling that I was moving toward more aliveness.

This was a time of leave taking. I had stayed overlong. All the residue of regrets about the past, the lack of certainty of the future, all the terrible losses, grievances, and hurts could not hold me back. It wasn't so much fear of failure, but fear that whatever I did next, whomever I was becoming might be mediocre. I didn't try to override the fear. Daily, I worked with it, allowing it to be there until it transformed and softened, was less needy, until I understood it well, until I could say with full integrity, "I love you. You are safe with me."

The day I submitted my resignation letter, now more than ten years ago, I felt a mix of dread, elation, and terror. Deeper still, I knew that I was being called to braver things, to living into a part of life that I could not completely understand or even articulate. I was being called out of the security of full-time work with its perks and problems and into living my soul's calling. I had taken the risk, and I was opening, blooming like a flower. I cherished the moment full of possibility, full of hope. I wasn't at all sure what the outcome would be, but the moment made sense.

The ongoing journey toward this emerging aspect of my life is supported by noticing life transitions, like noticing the transition from the midseason of late spring to summer. Life transitions are, in part, about letting go and letting come— honoring, grieving what I've left behind, making visible and conscious what is seeking to be birthed, including what might be difficult to accept.

* * *

It's spring again, 2021, and I am in a season of transition once more. A few months ago, my second divorce was finalized. Looking back, I understood that the marriage ended as unloving between us grew. I realized that our differences went beyond solely our race and gender; they included our values and vision of how to live. The marriage was choked out by sadness, isolation, and an unresolved love.

During an excessive-heat warning in July, he moved out. As he drove away, my heart shattered again into a million pieces. Looking back now, I see that this was a necessary ending laden with potential, much like the flower garden I had dreamed of creating. As a lawyer, I knew nothing about compassionate and loving divorce. I had a well-tended adversarial mindset that contributed to the marriage ending. Rather than ignoring or discounting the pit in my stomach that moved into the center of my chest and my heart, rather than trying to intellectualize my feelings, I began to allow myself to feel. I wanted to understand the sensations and what this "felt sense," the gut check, in my body was seeking to say about the marriage, the relationship, and me. The queasiness in my stomach was a dead giveaway and told me I was preparing for something, yet again, that I didn't want to do and wasn't at all sure that I could do. There was this nagging voice in the back of my head saying, *Dharma teachers don't get divorced. They live happy, contented, well-rounded family lives.*

Though a part of me wanted to hold on to the dismal and depressing marriage—because at least someone was there, at least I was not alone—I knew the marriage was already over, and I was already very alone. I had to come to this sad and yet important realization without deluding myself with wishful thinking, without hoping that somehow the situation would change, releasing false hope.

Again, this was a time of leave taking. Once I decided to seek a collaborative divorce and then chose a lawyer I greatly admired, the pit in the bottom of my stomach—the ache—stopped, replaced with hollow relief. I wasn't wishy-washy. I had chosen. There was no turning back.

Though I had reached the decision, I was consumed with the emotional turmoil of ending a fifteen-year interracial marriage that probably should not have happened in the first place. I arrived at my lawyer's office to sign papers, carrying fear, doubt, determination, resignation, and a strange hopefulness. Perhaps the saddest aspect was how little emotion was present. There was no crying for forgiveness, no begging to make things right again, nothing. Instead, the sad and familiar cold silence that had enveloped the marriage, moving us closer and closer to this moment, returned. I understood how coldness kills.

After the years of couples therapy, workshops, and books on relationships and more, I knew that the most loving and honest thing I could do was to choose divorce. This was a necessary ending, part of the life cycle of this marriage. Just as plants are pruned to promote new growth, to enhance the plant and encourage its growth and flourishing, the marriage had reached its natural life cycle. My work was to recognize that truth and, with love, let it go.

Close to the Jersey Shore, the lawyer's office was oddly cozy. Decked out with small bowls of Reese's Pieces, salted pretzels, and mini Mars bars, it offered comfort food for the troubled. The lawyer was a pro who had listened to these stories for decades. As I went to leave the office, she said to me, "You're creating your future now." In that moment, I didn't want to create the future. I needed to find something or someone to love me, to hold me, to witness the fragility of the moment, the brutish weight of suffering that brought me here.

I whispered to myself, "Darling, be generous with yourself. You know who you are." I then walked out into the afternoon sun, the parking lot landscaped with hardwood mulch and sense-numbing spirea and arborvitae. Instinctively, I knew I needed to be at the ocean, to lose my senses to the sound of the surf and the sky. I walked along the water, stood there a long time, and then walked the boardwalk, coming to a row of bathhouses. As I turned, my eyes caught graffiti on one of the doors: "This door is not an answer. It is a question"—a riff off Elie Wiesel's words in 1993 at the dedication of the US Holocaust Memorial Museum in Washington, DC. As I read the sign, I knew that not only was the door a question, I was a question, walking into the future I was creating.

> *Life will break you. Nobody can protect you from that, and living alone won't either, for solitude will also break you with its yearning. You have to love. You have to feel. It is the reason you are here on earth. You are here to risk your heart. You are here to be swallowed up. And when it happens that you are broken, or betrayed, or left, or hurt, or death brushes near, let yourself sit by an apple tree and listen to the apples falling all around you in heaps, wasting their sweetness. Tell yourself you tasted as many as you could.*
>
> —Louise Erdrich[3]

With all the change and losses of the preceding months, I set out in the spring, in the mud season, to reclaim my inner gardener, to water the seeds of peace, understanding, and love within me, to engage a theology of love. I began by replacing rotten wood and then painting my barnhouse. I removed diseased trees that threatened to fall on the house, cleared away heaps of junk, replaced the cottage roof, and painted over graffiti. I then turned to a small koi pond, which had been a source of joy but over the years, like the marriage, became stagnated.

Now the standing muddy water was overgrown with cattails and arrowheads, empty of fish. Shovel by shovel, I worked with a couple of friends and helpers to move plants and rocks, remove overgrown weeds, and reclaim the soil with organic matter.

Each month brought a new challenge in the garden: groundhogs, carpenter bees, wasps, and hard-as-rocks clay soil. While the garden was being reborn. I was being reborn.

On a sunny day in July 2021, after nearly one year of living unpartnered, I walked outside and looked at the place that just months earlier had been a hole in the ground with stagnant water. Now in its place were the sound of water from a glazed fountain and the sight of hummingbirds, butterflies, and goldfinches at my Nyjer seed feeder. There were bright blooms: pink *Echinacea purpurea*, feathery-white *Artemisia schmidtiana*, vivid red *Crocosmia* hybrid, and lemon-yellow *Coreropsis verticilata*. I went over to the giant staghorn fern and took it down from its hanger to give it a good watering. Days earlier, I had noticed that a tiny song sparrow had built a nest of pine needles behind the plant. As I put the nozzle deep into the cavity of the fern, I stopped. There, huddled together, lay five tiny brown-speckled eggs.

An often-quoted line from Emily Dickinson's poetry is "Hope is a thing with feathers."[4] It is birdsong. And it doesn't matter whether you appreciate it or not. Hope's job is to give and keep giving, without asking for anything in return, to shape and reshape the soul. In the Plum Village tradition, we are invited to wake up to suffering within and around us and hold suffering with care, to get to know suffering and to transform suffering into compassion, peace, and love. We are invited to cultivate a safe haven with each breath for ourselves and for all living beings. In the making of this garden, I was taught this transformation: to dig deep, deeper still, and to know that love is a digger.

* * *

Real love, true love, always involves pain, because no matter what is loved or how well, love will lead to transition, perhaps to an ending, certainly to change. That doesn't mean that I—that we—shouldn't love well. It means fighting like hell to hold on to the love that is here for as long as it is here, to cherish it with all our might, and then when wisdom calls for letting go, letting go. Letting go is a part of loving. And loving is about choosing to accept that letting go, eventually, is also how we love well.

In his song "Anthem," the singer-songwriter Leonard Cohen famously offered these lines:

> There is a crack, a crack in everything
> That's how the light gets in.[5]

We each have brokenness—broken open through loss, grief, and turbulence. I'm in this odd place of letting the "light get in" and accepting that love also includes cracks of grief and loss. I keep reminding myself that these cracks are how the light gets in. I have lots of doorlike questions: How do I love now? How do I believe in myself? How do I let the light in? How do I grow from the cracks?

The call to love, the risk to blossom like a flower garden, to be wildly brave *enough*—fiercely, passionately, courageously so. This is a time to declare my fragility and my strength, my faith and my power, my fearlessness and my fear. So I come back to this: Hope leans forward, always. It asks that we love hard and true. It asks that we release and let go wisely with compassion, with grace and kindness, because that's the right thing to do. And that's called big, true, brave love.

SEVEN FACTORS OF AWAKENING: THE FOURTH FACTOR, JOY

> *Joy must be one of the pivots of our life. It is the token of a generous personality. Sometimes it is also a mantle that clothes a life of sacrifice and self-giving. A person who has this gift often reaches high summits. He or she is like the sun in a community.*
>
> —Mother Teresa

Many of us think we need certain conditions to feel joy: the right partner, right job, right place to live, etc. We think if we get rid of our edginess, anger, or jealousy and replace it with another emotion, we'll be happy, joyful. When we think and act this way, we are, of course, replacing one craving for another, which doesn't work.

In the Plum Village community, we take good care of the sadness, isolation, loneliness, whatever strong emotion is arising, knowing that joy, like a flower garden, is cultivated.[6]

However, in the middle of a global pandemic, joy can feel like a tall order. I suggest that you start small. Start with delight. Consider the small glimmers of delight that you encounter in your daily life: waking up in the morning, wearing warm clothing, listening to your kids' laughter, connecting with a friend, cuddling with a pet. There are potentially countless glimmers of daily delight. Take a moment to savor them. Allow yourself to feel delight.

The Plum Village practice of connecting with delight— with what sparks joy and feeds us in positive ways—is called selective watering, watering the good within us to help it grow and flourish. The corollary in neuroscience is called experience-dependent neuroplasticity or taking in the good, a practice taught by the American psychologist Rick Hanson. He notes that experience matters[7]. We are constantly absorbing experience through our senses: eyes, ears, nose, mouth. However, too often we are unaware of the good that comes through our senses, that surrounds us in daily life. We live life as a flyby.

To practice taking in the good or selective watering is to cultivate joy, to become aware of the many delights of being alive, and to savor them even briefly. Thich Nhat Hanh recommended that we notice and then write down what brings joy and delight in our lives to savor these experiences. Mindfulness research makes clear that by doing this, we reinforce new neural pathways in the brain, and we activate oxytocin, commonly called the love hormone, said to be associated with feelings of love, belonging, and trust.

Real Voices, Real Courage

Along the way, we all need people who "get" us and whom we get. Susan Cross is that person for me. We met at a retreat I was leading at Ghost Ranch. I immediately recognized her as kindred soul and admired the parallel journeys through divorce and travel that our lives had taken. Here's what Susan has to say about braving your way forward in hope.

Susan Cross

She/her

Craftswoman (or crafts-crone), creator of shrouds, ritual tools, writing, and clothing

"Bravery, it would seem, is an ongoing willingness to face what you don't know."

I live in northern New Mexico, near the tiny village of Abiquiu, made famous by the nineteenth-century American painter Georgia O'Keeffe. There's a quote that's attributed to her: "I've been absolutely terrified every moment of my life—and I've never let it keep me from doing a single thing I wanted to do."

I think that's a good description of what bravery is; it's elevating truth over safety and stability and making choices based on truth. Bravery is reaching the end of your tether and letting the chips fall where they may. It's carrying a soul-load of fear, risk, worry, disillusionment, anger, and regret—and still attempting to get on with what must be done, like it or not.

An example of this in my life was my divorce. There were several hard years before the disintegration of all my carefully curated identities. It was a time of instability and fear of loss and change. For decades I'd been a wife, mother, educator, westerner. I was truly afraid to speak to my husband about our problems. I really had to struggle with my "internal sissy." Repeatedly I would screw up my courage, and over and over again, I would get cold feet and back down. Things had to get quite dire before my "bravery" overcame my dread.

When I finally told my husband that I didn't think our marriage was working anymore, every structure and pattern in my life disintegrated within a month. My marriage of twenty-five years ended. My daughter finished university and moved out on her own. I left my job. We sold our house. Suddenly, I didn't have a place, a family, or a purpose. I literally felt like I was in a vast, empty void. I felt pulled into a black hole, and I would actually feel a dropping sensation—a real, physical dropping sensation—in my body.

There are situations that there is no turning back from. That was honestly the hardest part—the deep realization that there was no reparation, no possibility of reconciliation. The intense being-in-a-void sensation went on for about six months. Literally, I felt there was nothing holding me together. I felt scattered across the universe and balled up in a badger's den at the same time. The Irish poet John O'Donohue describes that suffering "unhouses" you.[8] I intensely felt unhoused and purposeless. I had gone from one hundred miles an hour of responsibility at my job and in my family to absolute zero. It was a huge adjustment.

Sometimes I just cried. I slept a lot. To stay sane, I planned a year of wandering, hoping through travel to find myself again (whatever that means) as well as an appropriate place to resettle. For about two years, I pursued my ancestors and ancestral landscapes. I roamed and stayed with friends and family. I helped my brother, who I hadn't seen in twenty years, through an illness. I tried to remind myself that there were other worlds, other paths, other ways to frame my being and my purpose. I took courses and traveled to where I might grow and learn.

I spent time on the Isle of Erraid, which is on the west coast of Scotland. It's a little island associated with the spiritual community of Findhorn. It also happened to be near where my father's people came from. I thought I'd give living in a community a try, which I'd never done before. I found I liked living in community, sharing work and meals. I could also sense my Scots ancestors there; in fact, they made spontaneous contact with me.

From my past work as a place-based educator, I had a high interest in landscape and how landscape shapes people. I was more interested in the landscapes my people came from than the individual people themselves. I took the transition time to pilgrimage to not only Scotland but also Devon and Cornwall, where my mother's people were from.

Through these visits to ancestral landscapes, I developed a much greater appreciation of epigenetics. Many of the hardships experienced by our ancestors are carried forward in our DNA and trigger things in us; things like starvation or genocide, carry forward in traceable ways. You end up not only carrying the trauma of your people, but also carrying their strengths. Knowing that has been extremely powerful for me. I now have a very different appreciation for my talents, for my abilities to function in the world in all sorts of ways, and the strengths that I've been given. I'm very aware of and grateful for, not only the human flaws and frailties that come down my ancestral line, but also for the things that make me strong and brave. The Highland Clearances, the Potato Famine, the Cornish Rebellion—my ancestors lived through those horrible, politically induced times. Every group of people on the planet have been oppressed in some way, by somebody, at some time. So, it's not uncommon to be oppressed. One must be strong to live through a genocide. You have to be brave and resilient to immigrate to a country where you have no idea how you'll do or to stay behind and steadfastly survive. We're alive because those people were strong enough to endure. Bravery, it would seem, is an ongoing willingness to face what you don't know.

None of us get through life without experiencing substantial losses—lots of them, usually. We're all practicing for the ultimate letting go. The better you get with loss, the less frightening the void becomes. We never quite stop feeling the losses in our lives; we never quite heal from them all the way, and this is where compassion is required. Compassion for self and others emerges from loss.

Loss has been my greatest teacher. It has clarified my soul's desires, my sense of calling, my emergent awareness of my responsibility to my lineage. Loss, and responding to it, has given me a hard-won acquisition—the understanding that loss and courage never end, that growth is ungainly and scratchy, that there are currents in a life that are irresistible, that "happiness" is overrated, that stability is an illusion. Loss has given me the hard-won acquisition that we are not here for comfort, but to be heated and hammered, annealed and polished.

MINDFULNESS PRACTICE: CULTIVATING JOY
Time Required: 5 minutes or less

Reflect on something you have done that you enjoyed doing— something that brought you joy . . . something you did for another person . . . something you delighted in accomplishing . . . something someone else appreciated. Savor the moments of recalling this joy.

Describe what you did for that other person that brought you a sense of joy or delight. You might write this down or create an image of the moment. You might describe how it came about for you to do it. What resources did you gather to accomplish it? Was it simple or complex? How long did it take to complete it? Who benefited from this? Describe anything you did to make this happen. Notice how you feel as you recall what brought you delight and joy.

QUERIES

- In what ways have you learned to trust, to risk trusting the True Self, your soul?

- What is blossoming within you, what joy?

- How has the gift of vulnerability supported your spiritual journey, your growth?

Chapter 5

CULTIVATING WHOLENESS: THE BODY AS GROUNDED WISDOM

The body is our house—and how we live in it and where we occupy it are uniquely ours, as well as being part of the common human experience. The body is a treasure trove and an exquisite vehicle for our practice of waking up and being with what is.

—Jill Satterfield[1]

My grandmother, Lillian, like my mother, was a domestic and tough, but she also had a tender side. I absorbed her toughness more than her tenderness, even though I admired her tender side. When they came, the tender moments took me by surprise, and I cherished them. We had a ritual every week where she would get out the foot basin and the Wray & Nephew overproof white rum. My job was to wash and massage her feet with the rum. She believed white rum would cure her debilitating arthritis, and I felt special, being asked and sharing the time.

Her feet were muscled, boxer-like and built, evidence of a hard life of little ease. At that time, she was well into her seventies, youthful by today's standards, but back then, she was worn out, nearing the end of her life. Consciously or not, I absorbed many messages from this ritual. Two stand out. First, it's exhausting to be a Black woman; it runs your body into the ground. Second, self-care is essential, indispensable when life is hard. She deserved, she earned, this moment to care for herself and for her body.

This memory lingered in me when decades later, following an intuitive sense that I needed to care for myself in a different and unaccustomed way, I began studying Kundalini yoga. My work was punishing my spirit and my body, and I needed to find a way out of the mess. I had worked myself into uterine fibroid tumors that eventually contributed to several miscarriages. While I received medical treatment, there was no safe place for me to talk about what was happening to my body. I joined a support group for women who had experienced miscarriages, but I felt isolated as the only Black person in the group.

To heal myself from the pain, I created rituals of healing, much like my grandmother did with me. I attended retreats for women who had experienced miscarriage. I lit candles. I prayed. I read books on loss and grief. Yet all this and more couldn't dislodge the grief that had me like a straitjacket. It wasn't until I traveled to Japan on the eighty-eight-temple pilgrimage of Shikoku that I began to heal, an experience I described in my first book, *The Road That Teaches: Lessons in Transformation through Travel.*[2]

Our pilgrimage began in Osaka, and we took the high-speed train to Mount Koya, or *Kōya-san*, a World Heritage Site and the birthplace of Kobo Daishi, the founder of the Shingon school of Buddhism. The pilgrim officially begins at the temple gate at Koya as a symbolic act of commitment. Passing through the gate, the pilgrim takes a vow to complete the pilgrimage, not just for themselves but for the benefit of all beings. With moss-covered rocks, the scent of incense, the sound of temple bells and fast-moving water down forested hillsides, Mount Koya is a "thin place," where the material and spiritual world meet.

As I entered the graveyard and passed through the temple gate, I bowed. The cemetery was partly dedicated to Jizo Bodhisattva, the Japanese deity said to aid pregnant women and travelers. Jizo is the caretaker of deceased infants and children, including fetuses lost to miscarriage and abortion.

Hundreds of stone statues of Jizo line the cemetery stone walls. Some wear handsewn capes and hats, others stand atop mossy rocks, and still others receive a love note written in longing and loss. A damp teddy bear, a bouquet of faded flowers, yet another story of loss and love.

For years after the miscarriages and abortions, I felt barren and broken by the loss, shame, and guilt. There was a ragged, dispossessed part of me that I couldn't shake. Here in the cold spring dampness of *Kōya-san*, my loss and grief were acknowledged and shared, not by a handful of people sitting across a table in the basement of a hospital support group, but openly by a culture and a people. I sensed that those in the cemetery around me understood and, unlike the support group, made space for the grieving to be and to breathe. The Japanese people recognized and honored the grief of miscarriage and abortion through this cemetery and these healing rituals, which said to me, *What happened to you happened to us. What you've done, we've done. You are loved here. You can heal here. All of you is accepted, loved here.*

The loss from the miscarriages and abortions are still there, though less so; less chokingly devastating, but there. Looking back now, I realize that in some ways, the abortions and miscarriages were fueled by fear of further loss, of the uncertainty and fragility of relationships that held me back from loving and being loved. I kept second-guessing myself with questions: Was it my unrelenting drive to "succeed"? Was it the running from poverty and toward a legal career? Was it the years of weight training and intense exercise that had eventually molded my body into an impenetrable shape? The one thing I did know was that the healing I was seeking wasn't in the support groups with people comparing and one-upping their loss. The beginning of my healing started in a very unlikely place, halfway around the world in a cold, damp cemetery in Japan, where the collective grief was free to breathe and be held by everyone. With all this, I arrived at my first Kundalini yoga class: tough-minded and tough-bodied.

I started studying and practicing Kundalini yoga at about the same time I began studying meditation in the Plum Village tradition. Yoga and meditation were part of my healing process after a surgery for the uterine fibroid tumors, after my painfully short first marriage, and while pinned beneath the weight of my Big and Important Job as a lawyer-lobbyist.

As I began to practice yoga, one of my first realizations was that my breath and body were frozen and rigid, like a block of ice. I could barely turn my spine from left to right. My fingers dangled a couple of feet away from the ground as I folded my body forward, my hamstrings screaming with tension. Most shockingly, I couldn't feel my breath.

My years of living an intellectual, success-driven life set me up for intellectual breathing. I was largely in my head, cut off from the wisdom of my body. My breathing was frozen. I was so focused on "getting there" as opposed to "being there," and had spent so much time trying to outrun poverty and prove my own worthiness to myself and others that I had forgotten how to breathe. My breath, mostly in my upper chest, was shallow, and I recruited the secondary respiratory muscles of the neck, upper chest, and shoulders instead of the primary respiratory organ of the diaphragm, abdominal muscles, and the intercostal muscles between the ribs. I had forgotten how to breathe with my whole body.

In studying yoga, I recognized and acknowledged patterns from decades of living remotely in my body. In law school, I studied torts, evidence, commercial law, but I learned nothing about my body, the breath. And years of working hunched over a computer left me nearly inflexible in body and spirit. Though breathing fully and completely lies at the very center of life, I was stuck in a shallow pattern that mirrored my stressful life. With Kundalini yoga, I set out to reclaim my breath and my body.

Before I began Kundalini yoga, I experienced chronic pain in my jaw, upper back and shoulders, and sides of my neck from poor breathing and a habit of bracing myself, which even affected my mood. Unconsciously clenching muscles in the anal sphincter affected my back and shoulders. I was hypervigilant and impatient with a nasty edginess. Even today, when I have a flash of impatience, I still catch myself and notice that my breathing tracks the feeling in my body. I feel my breath weak and uneasy.

After my return from Japan, I began reading the books of Judith Hanson Lasater and Donna Farhi, long-time yoga teachers, and then took breathing-focused classes with them. In *The Breathing Book*, Farhi points to several important characteristics of "free breathing," which helped me understand the crucial, essential link between the mind, the body, and the breath.[3] It was time to practice, even though I had plenty of resistance and plenty of skepticism. I'd lie on the floor with my knees bent or resting the back of my knees on the edge of a chair and listen to myself breathe. I felt dumb, like "This is a total waste of time." I thought, "I could be squatting or dead-lifting weights. I could be walking seven or eight miles, uphill. What am I doing here?"

I'd force myself to lie there being still, waiting for something, anything to happen, waiting for a signal. I stuck with it, and after a couple of weeks of this "do nothing" breathing exercise, one day I felt something. It was my breath but not in my chest and shoulders. I felt it at my reproductive organs and below the navel. It was like my body was opening and closing to the rhythm of my in- and out-breath. Oscillating, at first the breath was moving my tailbone and then rolling upward and outward to my shoulders and hands and then downward and inward to my legs and feet. Like boneless seaweed, the breath moved higher and lower, left and right, circular and in, multidirectional, then becoming calm and effortless. Through quiet attention, patience, and perseverance, this bruised and battered part of my body was beginning to move in freedom and harmony.

Slowly, incredibly slowly, I was being invited to trust and allow the breath to emerge and to release naturally. As I practiced this "do nothing" breathing, these words came to me:

Allowing ease and release
Allowing body to soften
Allowing breath to know ease
Allowing kindness
Allowing in-breath to meet the out-breath
Allowing pause between the in- and out-breath
Allowing lungs to be free
Allowing belly to be free
Allowing the heart to be free
Rise
Fall
In

Out
Deep
Slow
Breath.

As I invited the breath, I was being invited to inquiry, not only about my body, but also about my hard-driving life, my values. As I began with this foundational breath and body awareness practice, I retrained how I was breathing. And as I did, a lot of my chronic neck and upper-back pain was alleviated. But more importantly, through the breath, the real me—the vital me, the whole me—was rediscovered. I had found a different kind of intellect, a wisdom from inside my body that felt whole and right.

* * *

"Do nothing" breathing is now one of my most important rituals and I offer it to individuals in my coaching and leadership work, as well as to groups on retreat. Several years ago, I was invited to open the annual conference of Spiritual Directors International with my dear friend Karen Erlichman, and we offered a version of the "do nothing" breathing. The grand ballroom was packed with maybe six hundred people all practicing the breath I stumbled upon at the height of disconnect from my body. Most people were standing with their hands on their belly, breathing. Some people were laid out on the stage flat on their back, eyes closed, following this essential breath back, way back to an essential part of themselves. Still others sat in chairs, gently swaying from side to side. It was beautiful. Here's what we did:

"Do Nothing" Breath Inquiry Practice

Choose what's best for your body to sit, stand, or lie down, and allow yourself to get in a comfortable position.

- Allow your eyes to be open or closed. Notice what feels most comfortable.

- Notice the shape of your body without judging yourself.

- Feel your feet on the floor if standing.

- Feel your legs, hips, torso, arms, chest, face.

- Allow your spine to relax, and become aware of the back, sides, and front of the body.

- Bring your attention to your breathing.

- Feel the breath come in and go out.

- Notice and feel the in-breath.

- Notice the pause between the in- and the out-breath.

- Notice and feel the out-breath.

- Feel the belly rise and fall.

- Practice gently bringing your attention back to the sensation of breathing; feel the rise and fall of your belly.

- Feel yourself breathing in and out.

- Imagine your body like boneless seaweed with roots, grounded yet totally free.

- Notice how you're feeling physically, mentally, emotionally, and spiritually.

- Take a moment to sense your breathing and ask yourself, "Where do I feel my breathing?" and simply wait.

- Return to the question over and over: "Where do I feel my breathing?" Let whatever perceptions you have be here without editing them. Don't discount tiny movements.

- Place one hand on the belly and the other at the chest or any place on your body, if that's appropriate for you, and feel the movement of the hand at the belly and at the chest or that part of your body.

- Ask yourself, "What does my breath feel like?" and simply wait without judging yourself. Gently keep returning to this question: "What does my breath feel like?" Become aware of words or images that might arise to describe your breath. Again, let whatever perceptions you have be here without editing them.

- Return your attention to the body and mind, gathering an impression of how you are doing at this moment. There is no need to change or edit this moment.

- When you are ready, stretch gently to close this practice and notice how you feel.

When I am doing "do nothing" breathing, or sometimes throughout the day, I pause even for a few seconds to ask myself:

- Where is the breath most noticeable?

- What is the frequency of my breath? Am I breathing fast or slow?

- What is the length of the in-breath, and what is the length of the out-breath?

- What is the texture of the breath? Is it smooth or rough?

- Is the breath shallow or deep?

- What is the quality of my breathing? If I were to describe my breath with words or images, what would I say?

I could be standing washing dishes at the kitchen sink or bent over cleaning a toilet. It really doesn't matter. I've trained myself to notice not just myself moving from one thing to the next but also the condition of my breath and body from the inside.

Through the Plum Village and Kundalini yoga communities, I've learned the art of slow, conscious breathing, which the writer James Nestor calls another name for prayer. I was learning to pray in a new and different way: to breathe and to be. Through the breath, I was learning that the personal patterns of uptightness and fear were mirrored back in my breathing and could be changed. I was learning to soften, to allow.

My grandmother had little chance to practice "do nothing" breathing. Yet our ritual of washing her feet with white rum taught me that you've got to make doing nothing a major priority, no matter what. And I do and will continue to practice that for her now.

Practice Being vs. Doing

Try this practice:

- Sit quietly for three to five minutes in an uncluttered private space in an inviting outdoor environment.

- Connect with your breath and any sensation in your body. Or if that doesn't feel right, connect with your external environment—the sky, for example.

- Scan your body for any tension and soften your body and your thoughts by gently releasing and dissolving the tension.

- Without forcing or trying to make anything happen, simply breathe and be for a few moments in this environment.

- Notice this as a moment of tranquility without having to make anything happen.

SEVEN FACTORS OF AWAKENING: THE FIFTH FACTOR, TRANQUILITY

Our capacity to relax, releasing layers of tension in the body and mind, is connected to tranquility. The first movement toward tranquility is stopping and pausing. When we pause, we settle into what's happening now in order to be present to what is. Think of tranquility, the pausing, as taking a warm bath. As we sink into the warm water, we begin to learn to recognize that we carry tension in the body and mind. We then pause, relax, and open or accept, as we meet the moment as it is. This kind of attunement and attentiveness allows softening and settling.

Real Voices, Real Courage

Brian Braganza is a colleague, a facilitator with the Center for Courage & Renewal. I invited him to speak with me because I was curious about his self-described identity as a brown man living in Nova Scotia, a predominantly white province, and how this affects his life and work. I have long admired Brian for his openhearted, body-centered approach. Here's what Brian Braganza told me during our conversation.

Brian Braganza

He/him

Consultant, facilitator, change maker

"First it's the feelings of apprehension, then the knowing that I have to act, then the fear arises again as I realize what I need to do, and then I dig in to find the courage or the bravery."

Bravery is about tapping into my integrity as a person. I have to find the bravery to do what I'm called to do, even if it feels like it's really going to challenge me, it's going to be really uncomfortable, or it's going to make me fearful. Often it feels like I don't have an option to back out because my commitment to my own integrity is telling me, "You've got to do this thing, Brian, whether you want to or not. It's the right thing to do." It's often the feelings of fear and anxiety that come up first, not the courage to act. The courage to act comes up later. First it's the feelings of apprehension, then the knowing that I have to act, then the fear arises again as I realize what I need to do, and then I dig in to find the courage or the bravery. Or if they don't come, sometimes I just fumble through it.

One particular place—this is really present for me right now—is with my mother, who was recently diagnosed with dementia. I've known for years, since my dad died in 2017, that something's not right. If not for my persistence the past few years, despite my fears, despite my mother's confusion about her situation, despite my sister's denial that there is anything wrong, we wouldn't have received a diagnosis. So even though I knew the outcome would not be positive, it was up to me to book appointments with specialists, follow up with doctors to have her driver's license revoked, and seek the information we needed to support her declining cognition, so that she can be safe and so I can support her in a healthy way.

It's not that anybody is telling me I had to do these things; it's an internal voice. I'm called to take these actions even though they produce anxiety and apprehension. I'm having really difficult conversations with my sister, who is taking a long time to come to terms with the disease and what my mother needs, which brings up a lot of anxiety and pain. And yet it's the right thing to do.

This sense of knowing the right thing to do, despite the fears, has been with me for much of my life. I often describe myself as an extreme introvert, yet my work is facilitating transformational spaces for individuals to grow into their whole self and then influence their communities. While it's absolutely the right work for me to do and it's my calling, I'm anxious nearly every time I get up in front of a new group. Yet I can't *not* do this work. While I've tried other vocations, I always get drawn back to this deep personal and social change work. I know I have a gift to bring.

I want my work to help make the world to be a better place, though I realize that's a pretty lofty hope. Part of my work is in collaboration with a therapist, where we provide an experiential therapeutic and wellness program to support men's mental health. This work involves disrupting the harmful messages of masculinity that keep men stuck, preventing them from taking care of their own mental health. This often leads them to inflict pain on themselves, their partners, families, and communities. As a small brown man often in very white groups of men, I'm afraid of the harmful messages of masculinity that might exist in these men—and in me. I'm afraid of the potential for harm and aggression toward me. And I have to face these fears to do the work I'm called to do.

There's this calling within, but there's also an external call. When I see some of the violence that some men perpetrate on others, I want to make a difference. In this work with men, I see how shifting the dominant story of masculinity makes a positive difference for the men, their partners, their children, and their communities. I know I'm doing transformative work that will ripple out in ways I'll never know.

What I've found in doing the masculinity work is that if men are given facilitated spaces, built around safety and healthy risk-taking, this gives them permission to be more of themselves, to shift their beliefs, to consider what they say and how they act. I've seen these shifts in attitudes in the way they respect each other, the way they respect themselves, the way they respect the women and children in their lives. I find that men are hungry for these spaces where they don't need to fit a rigid masculine mold, where they get to be their *whole self*. Yet if there isn't this safety in the group, they won't take the risks necessary to be themselves. This tells me that if I can transform my fears to work *with* me, rather than *against* me, then I can continue to support men in this meaningful work to create social change.

I've never really seen myself as anyone with great courage. I identify as a brown man. My parents were from India. I was born in Nigeria. We moved to Germany for a couple of years before we came to Canada when I was four. I rarely use phrases like South Asian Canadian or Indian Canadian to describe myself, and I rarely say I'm an immigrant. I'm Canadian, and I'm brown. I remember my first day on the school playground in a very white small town in Ontario: as the only brown boy on the playground, I felt it as a painful moment.

As a young person, I had to learn two things early on. One was to try to not be noticed, which was really hard for a brown boy in mostly white schools. I had to try to hide my identity so I wouldn't get picked on, yet I couldn't really hide. So I didn't speak up much, I kept to myself; I'd minimize how much space I took up, in an attempt to be invisible. Teachers would say, "Oh, he's so polite. He's so nice. He smiles a lot. He's so quiet." I think that was my way of protecting myself.

Second, I learned that because of my skin color, things were going to be hard for me. And yet that deep call inside led me to believe that I was going to live my life anyway. As a young man in my twenties, I did a lot of traveling across rural and remote places in Canada. I didn't want to prevent myself from doing what my heart wanted. During these times, there was certainly fear and terror, there was potential for harm, for racism, or for aggression, and I didn't want that to stop the blossoming of who I was becoming. I couldn't *not* do those things. When I was twenty-four years old, I traveled to India to find connection and sense of belonging. I was devastated that I didn't find it, yet I had to make that journey. My integrity to who I was becoming called me to make that journey and would not be denied due to any fears or apprehensions I might have had.

Rural Nova Scotia, where I live now, is largely white, and after twenty-five years of being here, I have built a really strong reputation as a facilitator and change maker. I often get requests for work because of who I am—my experience and my reputation. At one time, I might have thought my world was going to be difficult, yet it has turned out to be very life-giving and inspired. And I still take risks to put myself out there in certain circumstances; I still show up in the uncomfortable places.

My parents were an important influence and role models in risk-taking and bravery. Through their own tenacity and hard work, they were noticed by the owner of the company my mother worked for and were given an opportunity to move to Germany. They left India when they were in their late twenties, and my mother was four months pregnant. In 1961, with a limited ability to speak the language, they moved to a very small town, Rehau, on the border of East Germany. They were the only brown family in this town, and my sister was the first brown baby born in the town.

I often think about their courage and the risk they took at that time. They didn't tell their families that my mother was pregnant, because they knew that their families would want them to stay in India. Even though neither of them could speak German, my mother took a job as a translator from German to English while my father started training into management with the company. They must have had such confidence and bravado to say, "We're going to leave everyone and all we know behind and do this work in a country where we don't know the language." Eventually they were given an opportunity to come to Canada, where my dad opened and managed a plant here in 1968.

My parents had this intrinsic bravery and courageousness. They had confidence; they knew they belonged in Germany, in Nigeria, in Canada. They knew they had a right to pursue their dreams for their children. They didn't see their race as a barrier to what they wanted to do in the world, and they did really well for themselves. I'm grateful for the choices they made, and I'm grateful that I've had the opportunities I've had. I carry with me some of their confidence and bravery, which put them in really challenging situations. These days my mother has little memory of those early times with my father; she's forgotten our family stories in these countries, and her world is circling ever smaller. Yet her courage is still so present, like it's ingrained in her being.

In 2017, my father fell in the bedroom and couldn't get up, and my mother called the ambulance. He had been in the hospital for seven days before my mother told me what had happened. She didn't want to worry us. Immediately I called the hospital and spoke to a doctor to get more information, and then I got on a plane to travel to Brockville. I spent that first week talking to multiple doctors to try to figure out what was going on with him. They finally determined that he'd had numerous strokes since 2011, that he had vascular dementia and his body was shutting down.

I'd never navigated medical systems, but I found the bravery and confidence to figure it out. I had no choice. I'd show up early every day and wait for the doctors to come so I could talk to them and try to find out more information. I tried to keep my mother informed, though I could tell she wasn't fully grasping the situation.

It got to the point where he had to be moved into palliative care. It was up to me to communicate to my dad what was going on. Though he probably knew at some level, I looked him in the eyes and said, "We're moving you to another place, and this is where you will die." By then he couldn't speak at all, so he raised his eyebrows to indicate he understood. That's probably the moment in my life where I really had to dig deep to find courage and a lot of love, compassion, and gratitude for all that he'd given me. As my mother wasn't in a place where she could fully understand what was happening, it was my role to be there for him.

In this time now with my mother, it feels similar. It's my role to communicate to her that she has dementia and to help her process what this means. It comes back to my realizing that, despite the fears, I will have the difficult conversations and take the difficult steps and then find the capacity and courage, because the only choice I have is to do the right thing.

MINDFULNESS PRACTICE: THE BODY SCAN

Time Required: 10 minutes or less

In a mind-numbing, fast changing world, grounded awareness is more important than ever before. The body scan, a mindfulness practice of awareness and progressive relaxation, is a way of recognizing and releasing pent-up tension in the body to calm and soothe, restoring a sense of peace. Practicing the body scan is like giving your body a big hug. Here is the sequence of the practice.

Prepare. Prepare a quiet space where you will be undisturbed and have a pillow and blanket for support. Place the pillow in a way that is comfortable for you, and if you like, cover yourself with a warm blanket. The body scan can be done sitting, standing, or lying down.

Pause. Take a few moments to pause, sitting in a chair, standing, or lying flat on the floor. Bring your awareness to your entire body, and to the places where your body touches the floor or the chair. Feel the air around you. Become aware of the entire body, from the crown of the head to the bottom of the feet.

Notice. Notice where you feel your breath. Exaggerate the breath for a moment, feeling the sensation of the breath coming in and going out, feeling the rise and fall of the belly and the chest expand and contract.

Open. Open your awareness, without becoming entangled, to sensations *internally* in the body: heat or coolness, numbness, tiredness, whatever is present.

Open your awareness, without becoming carried away, to sensations *externally* around you, to sound, silence, smells, sensations where your body comes in contact with the chair or the floor.

Relax. Release tension gently, accepting yourself with kindness and allowing the body to be alert and yet tranquil, not sleepy. Gently soften the body without pushing anything away—allowing everything to be as it is, like an ocean tide coming in and going out or a door opening and closing, noting that this is how it is now, acknowledging what is already here, meeting tension with kindness, softening.

Connect. Connect with the stability of the ground underneath you. Connect with the space around your body. Connect with warmth and the sense of your body, your heart, and your belly.

Feel. Notice whatever sensations are present.

Feel the crown of the head, the face, the eyes, ears, nose, mouth, tongue, teeth, lips, and the front, sides, and back of the head.

Feel the neck—front, sides, and back. Feel the chest, lungs, heart, torso, sides of the body.

Feel the arms, front and back, and each finger.

Feel the back of the body from the back of the neck through the upper, middle, and lower spine.

Feel the belly, navel center, stomach, the digestive and reproductive organs. Feel the buttocks and legs—the side, back, and front of the legs and knees.

Feel the feet and toes.

Feel the entire body—front, back, and sides.

As you bring the practice to a close, breathe deeply and stretch.

QUERIES

- How do you recognize and express gratitude for the gift of your body and this life?

- What can you do to support greater awareness of your body?

- What does your body's own wisdom teach you about yourself, your feelings, and your emotions?

Chapter 6

DEEPENING CONNECTIONS: JOURNEYING WITH COMMUNITY, MENTORS, AND FRIENDS

We never know how our small activities will affect others through the invisible fabric of our connectedness. In this exquisitely connected world, it's never a question of "critical mass." It's always about critical connections.

—*Grace Lee Boggs*

As a teacher at Pendle Hill outside Philadelphia, I continue to grow in my understanding of community. A safe, brave space, Pendle Hill is where, on my better days, I bring my most compassionate self forward. This compassion spirals outward as an invitation—an invitation that inclines others to do the same. In this community, I learn about connection and about sharing my vulnerability in ways that grow me, that grow others.

These lessons are iterative and, through an accumulation of moments of adding to, adding again, enlarge me and, through me, others. Recently, I offered an online Dharma talk for a group of mostly BIPOC social activists in Baltimore, Maryland. In the talk, I invited these seasoned activists to "map their love story" of how they came to love the work of social justice: Who were the people and what were the places and events that changed their lives that brought them to activism?

As I extended the invitation, I shared an example in my own life. I spoke about Harriet and Ruby, Black chefs at an ornate yet slightly worn out, Southern-style gingerbread Victorian hotel in Cape May, New Jersey. Harriet and Ruby were famous for their fried chicken and biscuits, which they had learned to make from their mother, Miss Eloise, who was the head chef at the hotel for decades. When I met them, they had been making chicken and biscuits for more than fifty years at the hotel, and had been widely acclaimed by the governor and various local and national celebrities who came to Cape May. For years, I was a devoted volunteer, making an annual journey to the hotel to paint, scrape, spackle, sweep, wash, and garden with others from around the country to help preserve the place and to keep the staff, including Harriet and Ruby, in the work they loved.

One day, I stopped into the kitchen to find Harriet with one hand on her hip and the other hand gently turning fried chicken with a slender two-pronged fork in a massive cast-iron fry pan and Ruby rolling biscuits. I paused in the moment to take in the chefs and the scene, and I asked them what's the most important thing they learned about cooking from Miss Eloise. Without missing a beat and without even looking up from the fry pan and table full of dough, they said practically in unison, "Love. You've got to put love in everything you do. People can taste it."

That moment stayed with me. Acting from a place of love is risky, yet we're made for it. As I invited the group to consider their own influences and invitations, I spoke about Harriet and Ruby and my own invitation to work in social justice. When I risk showing up undefended, open, and accessible, I create dynamic conditions for others to do the same. Love is an invitation you accept as gift. It comes with a learned commitment to preserve it and pass it on. Offering one another loving presence is a spark that catches fire, igniting us with greater bravery and courage.

Now, as I reflect on the inspiration of Harriet and Ruby, I know that it was love. Love drew me and other volunteers into the community that supported the hotel by painting, scraping, cleaning, and spackling. It was love that grabbed me by the hand toward the work of social justice. It was love at my back that brought me into the Plum Village community, Ghost Ranch, and Pendle Hill.

It's easy to have idyllic beliefs about community—that it is a place where everyone is friendly, agreeable, and polite; a place where there is no conflict, connection is easy, there are no difficult people. What I've discovered, however, is that more often than not, community is about conflict and about how we together navigate it. Conflict often reveals something important, allowing me to yield to something bigger and more important than protecting my ideas around right or wrong. Community calls me toward recognizing the shadow side of myself: the ways in which I am hard, distant, rigid, and unforgiving. Community shows me when I am placing my needs before others, showing up distracted or late, and taking others for granted. The opportunity I am then given is to ask essential questions: Can I be transparent and undefended without collapsing when this feedback comes my way? Can I notice, name, and investigate with open curiosity what I am feeling? Can I offer myself and others kind attention without judgment or blame? The gift of community is the mirror that reflects back to me, that offers me a chance to live into a better part of myself.

But what happens when community with a sense of real connection is hard to find? My neighbor Lilybelle comes to mind. For a long while and with the global pandemic, Lilybelle's sense of true connection to herself and to others was TV and an occasional Zoom get-together with her grown kids, who lived far away. At first, the solitude was welcome, a break from event-packed days. But after weeks of social distancing, solitude became isolation, and then loneliness affected her mood and motivation. One time when I called her, she said she struggled with a loss of energy some days, had trouble sleeping, and knew she was eating way more than she should without exercising. Her only regular human contact was the Amazon driver making breathless stops. She told me, with an embarrassed laugh, she found herself wanting the drivers to linger, even for a couple of minutes, just to talk.

It had been weeks, maybe months since Lilybelle connected with the tender touch of another living thing. At the urging of some of the neighbors, including me, she adopted a cat, Peaches, as a rescue from the animal shelter. Peaches fit right into her solitary life and condo. Within a couple of days, Peaches was snuggling in her lap as Lilybelle sat in her favorite chair and was waking her up in the morning, stretching and purring for attention. Reflecting on the new companion, Lilybelle felt good inside—the sense of affection again, the warm glow of connection.

Loneliness and Community

Many of us knew long before COVID-19 the truth of Surgeon General Vivek Murthy's 2017 statement declaring loneliness an "epidemic" and a "public health crisis." The warning came on the heels of several studies that underscored the true impact of loneliness not only on the body but also on the mind.

In 2018, a study funded by the Kaiser Family Fund reported that more than a fifth of adults in the United States (22 percent) claimed "they often or always feel lonely, feel that they lack companionship, feel left out, or feel isolated from others, and many of them said their loneliness has had a negative impact on various aspects of their life."[1] The same study revealed that "loneliness is felt disproportionately by people with lower incomes and those with debilitating health or mental conditions." Those who reported loneliness said that they have "few or no relatives or friends living nearby who they can rely on for support" and have few meaningful connections with family, friends, and neighbors.

A similar study in 2020 by the National Academy of Sciences, Engineering, and Medicine found that social isolation and loneliness are serious and underappreciated public health risks, affecting a significant portion of Americans ages sixty-five and older[2]. In a study published in 2015, the researchers found that actual and perceived social isolation are associated with increased risk for early mortality—having harm equivalent to smoking fifteen cigarettes per day.[3]

Community—meaningful connection—doesn't just feel good; it's a biological imperative. We cannot survive without it. That's something Lilybelle knew when she decided to bring a cat home from the shelter. And that's something I learned when I rebuilt the garden at my home outside Philadelphia, with friends coming alongside me in the hurt of loneliness. This isn't about objective social isolation, either. The studies show the *perception* of loneliness is lonely. We all need social connection, social interaction, and companionship for the thriving of ourselves and others.

As a single person living alone, sometimes when I am in the grip of feeling alone and want to seek out togetherness in community, I can be under the illusion that in community I'll find only people I like and who like me back. Yes, the gift of community includes the people who model compassion, generosity, and kindness and invite me to do the same. Yet perhaps the truest gift of community comes in the people who are very different from me, the people I find most challenging.

Parker Palmer, in writing about community, shares an important truth:

> In true community we will not choose our companions, for our choices are so often limited by self-serving motives.

Instead, our companions will be given to us by grace. Often they will be persons who will upset our settled view of self and world. In fact, we might define true community as that place where the person you least want to live with lives . . . .

Community will teach us that our grip on truth is fragile and incomplete, that we need many ears to hear the fullness of God's word for our lives. And the disappointments of community life can be transformed by our discovery that the only dependable power for life lies beyond all human structures and relationships.[4]

In community, I've learned to shift my focus from what I think the other person is doing that I find wrong or irritating, which keeps me in narrow, self-centered blame or shame, to modeling how I want to be treated with kindness and care. It's easy to focus on what I don't like or don't want and harder to ask for what I do want. From years of studying mindfulness in the Plum Village community and with Thich Nhat Hanh, I am trained to notice assumptions and to ask myself these powerful questions: "Are you sure?" and "What do you really want out of this interaction, this relationship?" Acknowledging that what's happening may not be what you had planned creates an atmosphere of learning for ourselves and for everyone and offers people a chance to be accountable and then create new choices.

Community as Safe Space, Brave Space

As a facilitator and Dharma teacher, I work with diverse groups and often in retreat. People come together for an event that might meet for under two hours or for more than one year. Many arrive as strangers, feeling apprehensive, yet they are seeking community—to share the intimacies, the yet-unrevealed common bonds of their lives, to learn trust. My work is, in part, to hold brave space, to create a sense of trust and emotional and psychological safety, and a dynamic, emergent, and transformative space for people to open as they choose, to take risks to be their authentic selves. I am asking communities of people gathered in retreat to lean into discomfort that foreshadows transformation. I am inviting them to enter messiness that can create authentic relationships, to release the idea that we will be perfect, and to move at a human pace: the speed of trust.

In 2014 I learned about bringing people together in community while studying Council Practice at the Ojai Foundation in Ojai, California. An ancient practice sourced in cultures across the globe and in classical Greek culture, Council Practice supports group interaction, conflict resolution, storytelling, decision-making, and co-visioning. It provides a primary tool for building community alongside mindfulness practices, like mindful awareness and mindful speaking and listening. In Council, people come together to sit in a circle and speak and listen to each other about the intimacies of their lives.

From the time I learned Council Practice, I began infusing my work with groups with the practices. Over several summers, for example, I offered Council Practice at an international high school in Connecticut, where I worked as a mindfulness teacher. Students attending an intensive, life-changing summer program incorporated Council Practice, outdoor adventures, filmmaking, public speaking, leadership skill building, and mindfulness practices. The program concluded with an overnight silent retreat. During the summer program, I sat in circle with teens from around the globe, passing a "talking piece," an instrument offered to unite the group and focus attention as it is passed from participant to participant in the circle. The person with the talking piece was invited to speak as we had the honor of offering the speaker our deepest listening, with attention, awareness, and with the intention of avoiding judgment.

At Ojai I learned to be fully present, to pay attention to the energy being co-created in the moment, to witness each person in their full humanity. The practice encourages us to shift focus from the mouth of the speaker to their heart, knowing that the person speaking was not just offering words but communicating a truth from the heart. Practices like this that build community take courage. To bring people together in small or large groups and to invite them to trust themselves and trust people they don't know is a profound act of generosity, hope, and courage.

I've found two very important ways to create trust and belonging within small and large communities. The first is through building a set of community agreements or group norms. The second is in offering people opportunities to share about these agreements or group norms and, more vulnerably in smaller groups of two or three, to speak as they wish about their lives, knowing that a foundation for safety is created through the agreements.

Community Agreements

Community agreement models may evolve and change based on the group and the group's needs and composition. Some groups, because they are coming together just once and for a very short time, might need to be reminded of the guiding principles that help create brave space, such as the agreement for confidentiality within the group.

My experience in working with busy people, especially with leaders, is that many people have little time to reflect on their values that brought them to their work and how those values align with their work. Our daily life is consumed with the essentials of work, caring for family, and everyday routines. Reflection gets squeezed out. Yet when people gather intentionally in groups, the agreement around safe space, brave space, and confidentiality is important to aid that reflection.

When groups are looking for resources, I often refer them to the Center for Courage & Renewal's Touchstones as a way to begin exploring how to be in community with each other. The Center for Courage & Renewal aims to engage people worldwide in courageous, compassionate, and authentic conversations through the use of its Touchstones in a process of group reflection called the Courage & Renewal Approach or Circle of Trust. The Center for Courage & Renewal's mission is to assist people to live more authentically, joining their soul with their role in the world. The following Touchstones, developed by the center's cofounders and Parker Palmer, are agreements that the center developed as a starting point.

Circle of Trust Touchstones for Safe and Trustworthy Space

Give and receive welcome. People learn best in hospitable spaces. In this circle we support each other's learning by giving and receiving hospitality.

Be present as fully as possible. Be here with your doubts, fears and failings as well as your convictions, joys and successes, your listening as well as your speaking.

What is offered in the circle is by invitation, not demand. This is not a "share or die" event! Do whatever your soul calls for and know that you do it with our support. Your soul knows your needs better than we do.

Speak your truth in ways that respect other people's truth. Our views of reality may differ, but speaking one's truth in a Circle of Trust does not mean interpreting, correcting or debating what others say. Speak from your center to the center of the circle, using "I" statements, trusting people to do their own sifting and winnowing.

No fixing, saving, advising or correcting each other. This is one of the hardest guidelines for those of us who like to "help." But it is vital to welcoming the soul, to making space for the inner teacher.

Learn to respond to others with honest, open questions. Instead of counsel and corrections. With such questions we help "hear each other into deeper speech."

When the going gets rough, turn to wonder. If you feel judgmental or defensive, ask yourself, "I wonder what bought them to this belief?" "I wonder what they're feeling right now?" "I wonder what my reaction teaches me about myself?" Set aside judgment to listen to others—and to yourself—more deeply.

Attend to your own inner teacher. We learn from others, of course. But as we explore poems, stories, questions and silence in a Circle of Trust, we have a special opportunity to learn from within. So pay close attention to your own reactions and responses, to your most important teacher.

Trust and learn from the silence. Silence is a gift in our noisy world, and a way of knowing in itself. Treat silence as a member of the group. After someone has spoken, take time to reflect without immediately filling the space with words.

Observe deep confidentiality. A Circle of Trust depends on knowing that whatever we say will remain with the people to whom we choose to say it—whether in a small group or in a large circle—and will never be passed on to others without our explicit permission.

Know that it's possible to leave the circle with whatever it was that you needed when you arrived, and that the seeds planted here can keep growing in the days ahead.

The Touchstones are akin to a boundary marker, especially for those feeling unsure and unsettled. They promote mutual respect and accountability, create expectations of how to treat one another and how to address conflict. When I'm facilitating a first gathering of a group, when we are in the critical formative stage, we spend time reading and discussing them. We break into smaller groups to talk about the guidelines, and we invite quiet time for individuals to write and reflect on them.

We talk about where we feel at ease with the Touchstones and which ones may challenge us. We might fall short with the Touchstones and how we need to be with ourselves and with each other when this happens. Again, brave space is not about perfection.

The Touchstone of "No fixing, saving, advising or correcting each other" is particularly challenging for most people. I've found that one of the strongest impulses for many people, including me, is to problem-solve, the opposite of "no fixing." I see this at play in retreats, facilitating groups, and especially in my role as codirector of the leadership coaching program at Georgetown University's Leadership Coaching Program. Many students are current or former highly paid corporate executives with an overcharged problem-solving mindset, ostensibly from years, maybe decades of fixing things: people, systems, etc. They enter the leadership coaching program and come face-to-face, perhaps for the first time, with understanding how, despite good intentions, problem solving actually backfires, how it interrupts a person's innate inner wisdom, and how it undermines trust in another's capacity to make appropriate choices for themselves.

Now, rather than problem solving for others, these coaches-in-training learn to partner with another through presence, open questions, empathetic listening, strategic use of silence, and more that invites the person to trust their own insight, their own learning and growth in the undefended, dynamic presence of the coach partner. Like the Touchstones, coaching creates brave space to accept ourselves and others as whole, resourceful, and creative. We are not broken and in need of fixing, saving, or correcting. We each have inner wisdom, an Inner Teacher we can trust.

Coaching and these Touchstones developed for groups reveal the deeper implications of trust. To better equip ourselves and others to listen to this inner wisdom, I coach students and groups to notice what's happening within them and around them and to seek ways to slow down, to limit distractions, to care for themselves in body, mind, emotions, and spirit. We do the "inner work" of self-reflection to do the "outer work" of our lives.

We begin Circle of Trust community gatherings and retreats with welcoming rituals to signal the start of something new. Chairs are set in a circle. A small bouquet of seasonal flowers rests on a center table. A cloth is draped across a table, suggesting attention and care. Inspirational quotes may be posted around the room, again to say, "You came to the right place. You are welcome here." A candle is lit, signaling transition into community time, a new beginning, as people enter the room and take seats around the circle. Laughter may be heard in one corner of the room, and others are in curious conversation. As a way of creating connections, I invite small groups of twos and threes to gather and begin talking about what brought them to the retreat. The group begins the movement from outsider to insider, to integral, to the community.

> *All real living is meeting.*
>
> —*Martin Buber*

Community as Vulnerability

> *The only choice we have as we mature*
> *is how we inhabit our vulnerability.*
> —*David Whyte*

> *To be alive is to be vulnerable.*
> —*Madeleine L'Engle*

To be in community is an act of vulnerability, to risk being misunderstood for the sake of understanding. To be vulnerable is to be permeable, porous to life, to our body and feelings, to others. Rather than standing apart and distant, we allow ourselves to be affected, to be open, and to connect. Community asks that we risk breaking our heart open, that we risk speaking and trusting.

It's that risk I took when I began traveling around the world in pilgrimage. And it's a risk that Lilybelle took, opening herself to another in her home, sharing space. Now it's been more than a year with Peaches, and Lilybelle is feeling very different about her life. Peaches' unconditional love, companionship, and physical touch have all made a huge difference in her outlook on life. I now see Lilybelle in the neighborhood on sunny days. She's back to reaching out to her kids on a regular basis and spending more time outdoors instead of in front of the TV, and that too has helped. Peaches has brought a renewed sense of connection back into her life, something for which Lilybelle is feeling grateful. Some days she still feels lonely, but this passes quickly. Connection, affection, and the touch of another living being are back in her life, and Peaches is part of building an inner sense of community, cultivated from within.

SEVEN FACTORS OF AWAKENING: THE SIXTH FACTOR, CONCENTRATION

To concentrate is to be intentional and purposeful, to give our full awareness in the moment. When we are concentrating, we reaffirm what is important. There is a settling, a gathering of attention to be here now, to awaken to what is just now, and to cultivate a motivation, an intention that is in service of creating a better world. Though openness, curiosity, flexibility, vulnerability, and acceptance are important to building community, so is concentration. It's through being aware, present, sensitive, responsive to another that we shape our daily interactions that build community. Concentration is not about analyzing, judging, or reporting from an emotional distance what you see and experience, but rather being, accepting at least for the moment whatever is happening without an agenda to change or fix things, cultivating a mind and heart of kindness, and then acting from that place.

Try this practice of concentration:

- Find a place outdoors and focus on one thing: the sky, an ant, a leaf.

- Allow your attention to focus on the object, much as you might shine a flashlight in a dark room.

- Notice when you get distracted, and then bring your attention back to the object.

- When you get distracted, offer yourself kindness and offer yourself space to return to concentration.

- After a few minutes, stretch and notice how you feel.

Among those who deftly practice concentration are poets. You may wish to read David Budbill's poem "This Morning," which speaks to the fleeting nature of attention and concentration. He begins the poem with a praise to the morning, to the present moment, "which I can turn into forever." He writes of how the forever moment is created by "loving what is here."[5]

Real Voices, Real Courage

Francisco Burgos, executive director of Pendle Hill, knows community. I've known Francisco since he arrived at Pendle Hill in 2017 and have admired his warmth and dedication to community. In our conversation, he shares about what brought him to Pendle Hill and his views on community.

Francisco Burgos

He/him

Executive director, Pendle Hill, a Quaker retreat and study center

> *"Bravery means acting with intentionality—with courage—despite the fears that we are facing."*

I describe myself as an educator, as somebody with a passion for learning and sharing that learning with others, and Pendle Hill, a Quaker retreat center outside Philadelphia, is a unique space for re-creation and learning. I came to Pendle Hill in 2017 to serve as the director of education. I had been here for workshops and for meetings. Before this time, I was living outside of the United States in a small rural community in Costa Rica, working for a small nonprofit as the director of the Center for Community Development. Before that, I was the director of a small Quaker school.

When I found out that Pendle Hill was looking for a director of education, I thought this would be a great opportunity, as my family was looking forward to returning to the US from Costa Rica. It was a natural fit for me, because as an educator, I wanted to be in a place where I could exercise my values in what I do every day. There were certain elements that spoke to me at that moment: I was going to be involved in the designing of programs that address social issues as a spiritual call, and there was a strong connection to my faith, values, and my beliefs.

Over the past five months, I have been serving Pendle Hill in a new role as the new executive director, a big transition. I believe that this organization has a lot to offer, so I applied for the position.

I am originally from the Dominican Republic. I grew up in a Catholic family in Santo Domingo, the capital of the Dominican Republic, in a low-income and marginalized community. Today that neighborhood is still low-income, and people are still facing many challenges associated with poverty. When I reflect on my personal history, I look to that place because I don't want to forget where I came from. I think that helped me to have clarity in thinking about how I can be a better person in the world.

Very early in my life, I was inspired to become a priest, so I went to seminary during my adolescent years and spent several years in seminary. I left the seminary for college and then for training as a clinical psychologist. I also taught at a school that was led by the Christian Brothers, a Catholic order dedicated to education, and I fell in love with that. I went back to seminary and continued as a brother for several years. And after that, I found that I needed to leave the order. When I did, I remained very close to the brothers, even today. Anytime, anywhere I go where there are brothers, I've found that connection, especially in the places where I used to live—Guatemala, Costa Rica, and the Dominican Republic. The brothers have never considered me an outsider, and I have never considered them different from my natural community. Being a brother was a big foundation of who I am. I recognize that this sense of community, service, and space for renewal and introspection are essential to me.

To me, being brave doesn't necessarily mean not having fear. Bravery means acting with intentionality—with courage—despite the fears that we are facing. Being brave is an act that is full of curiosity, is full of hope, is full of searching for the alternative and maybe the recognition that things can be different.

Several life stories describe how I have personally embraced this in my life. One of them has to do with my own transition here to the United States after I left the brotherhood. I was unemployed, but I had a friend who was working on a big project for the government of the Dominican Republic at that time, and he managed to put together a group of people for a major project, which involved a group ex-brothers and priests. Because this guy was very familiar with liberation theology and many of the activities that some of us were incorporating in working with communities, he put us together, and many practical projects were conceived, including the creation of a national mobile library system for the Dominican Republic.

Nearing the end of my work with that group, I worked on another project, where I met my future wife, Renee, who was a Peace Corps volunteer at the time. I was developing a hundred libraries in rural communities, and Renee was in one of those communities and was also interested in supporting the library at a public school in her community. This is how we connected, and our relationship developed. I had a great job. I was well paid, and the path to grow in that organization was amazing. I started getting more involved in the regional area and Central America and managed many of the financial projects, including projects in Haiti. It was a unique position. At the beginning of 2003, Renee's family in the US was going through a crisis that was taking a big toll on them emotionally and financially. I remember saying to Renee, "Hey, if your family needs you, we'll go." And she looked at me and said, "What?" Renee was working for another nongovernmental organization, and we each had found our dream jobs in the Dominican Republic.

At that time, in the early 2000s, the Dominican Republic was in an economic crisis, but instead of shrinking, my finances were growing. When I told my friends that we were leaving for the US, they said, "You are telling me that you are willing to lose this job that offers you space, financial security, and potential for growth?" And I said, "Well, if your family needs you, that's the right thing to do." In my family, the sense of unity and support was very strong. This is still important to my family. It was important to me to support my partner as she tried to help her family. This was the driving force.

So, we talked to Renee's family, and we made the decision that we would come to the United States and support the family. We were going to run the little family business, and I was going to find my way. The transition was hard. I had been very successful in my own country, I was a fully capable professional, and I was leaving everything behind. I belonged to a large family, and we got together every single Sunday. I was very involved with the cultural development in my city—literature circles, reading clubs, you name it. I was very invested in the life of my city, and at the same time, I was very supportive of certain projects that the brothers were doing. While I left the brotherhood, I continued working as a youth trainer. So when I look back at that situation, in saying yes to this transition, I was leaving that behind and walking into the unknown.

I was one of those rare people who never wanted to live in the US. I was not interested in coming to the US. I was not interested in learning English. Despite all that, we decided to move, and I never lost the audacity to keep moving even with the hardships.

When I arrived in the US, I wasn't able to find quality work. I couldn't have intimate conversations because I was unable to speak the language and express my feelings. At that point, I made the decision to study English. I began meeting people who shared my own history: highly educated professionals who were working in McDonald's. They were cleaning houses because they couldn't speak the language. After two years here in the US, negotiating the complex immigration system, I decided to go to graduate school, and I received a master's degree in sustainable development from the School for International Training in Brattleboro, Vermont.

Pendle Hill is a place that nurtures bravery. People come to Pendle Hill as an act of bravery because they allow themselves to go through spiritual discernment while being offered simple but radical hospitality to feel welcome without any prerequisite. They open themselves to processes that will be challenging, and several programs come to mind, like Journey Toward Wholeness, a year-long four-part retreat series based on the work of Parker Palmer and the Center for Courage & Renewal. The fact that the Catholic Association of Women Priests chose Pendle Hill is, to me, a statement of radical hospitality. This is the place and a community where people feel safe to explore whoever they are.

I want Pendle Hill to be a prophetic witness institution, to expand our radical hospitality. "We want to welcome you." That means we have to work internally, because it is very easy to support groups or individuals that are aligned with our values, but what happens when a white supremacist group wants to rent a space here?

Is exercising radical hospitality saying yes to everybody? Or is radical hospitality creating a space for good discernment about when to say no? Radical hospitality has to be in connection with that sense of being a prophetic witness institution. So, we keep creating space for prophetic possibility.

To my colleagues here at Pendle Hill, I say, "This is not my dream. This is our dream. Let's dream together, and let's encounter the many possibilities in front of us. I know we may fail in some of them, but how can we live the journey if we don't try it? How will we find our way if we don't work together to explore what Pendle Hill can continue to be for so many? Let's continue supporting opening Pendle Hill as a place to be and become."

MINDFULNESS PRACTICE: BEGINNING ANEW

Time Required: Varies
Participants: 2

Beginning anew is a process of reconciliation in community and comes from the Plum Village tradition.[6] The focus is not on asking for forgiveness when we've caused harm but instead is a way of understanding our actions and their effect on others. The process has three parts: flower watering, or expressing sincere and genuine appreciation for the other person; expressing regrets; and expressing hurts and difficulties. This practice can prevent feelings of hurt from building up and helps create safe and brave space in community. Often, the process is done between two people, and it can also be done with small groups.

Here's an abbreviated and modified version of the practice between two people.

Calendar space and time. Set aside time in your calendar for this practice. The Plum Village community engages in this practice weekly.

Set the physical space. Create a physical atmosphere of welcome, peace, and harmony through simple acts: a quiet, safe, and uninterrupted space, a flower, or element of nature, for example.

Flower watering. Take turns speaking without interruption about the positive qualities you see and experience in the other person; speak genuinely and sincerely.

Express "beneficial regret." There is a benefit we gain from having regret, learning from it, and resolving to do it differently, better next time. What do you regret about your actions? Again, take turns speaking and listening.

Express ways you have felt hurt by others. Speak in a way that is truthful and yet kind. Use "I" statements to share your perceptions and feelings. The listener practices listening for understanding rather than correction, listening to help alleviate the suffering in the speaker. The speaker and listener may decide to agree to not respond to anything that is shared until at least twenty-four hours later, when you meet again. Although it's sometimes hard to keep from responding in the moment, this guideline is very helpful in containing and taking care of reactions and impulses in the moment, especially when strong feelings arise.[7]

Hugging meditation. Yes, in the Plum Village tradition, even hugging another person is meditation! In this practice, you are really there, really hugging. It's not a perfunctory pat on the back. Instead, we look at the other person, bow deeply, and embrace while following three in- and out-breaths, and then we release, knowing that we have made genuine and heartfelt connection.

QUERIES

- What connections matter in your life?
- How do you nurture and protect the things, the people, the community, and the causes you care about?
- What challenges have you experienced in community or with others that have served your growth and learning?

Chapter 7

LIVING YOUR GENUINE: TRUTH TELLING TO EMBRACE THE TRUE SELF

There is something in every one of you that waits, listens for the sound of the genuine in yourself.

—*Howard Thurman*

On a day near the end of summer, while I was standing at the kitchen sink, looking out the window at the forsythia and a goldfinch feeding at the birdfeeder, a voice came to me, saying, "Stop everything. Stop." I looked around to see who was speaking. In a flash, I knew the inner voice was speaking a truth I needed but didn't want to hear. The truth is, I wasn't sure I knew how to "stop everything." As if turning my face away from a too-bright, glaring sun, I had been avoiding this moment of reckoning, a truth telling with myself.

This moment came long after I had quit my job as a lawyer-lobbyist, after taking the leap of faith to launch my coaching and retreat company. My work life was rich and robust beyond what I could have imagined. Actually, my work life was unsustainable. After the murder of George Floyd, I started getting a torrent of calls, invitations from companies and nonprofits around the United States to offer programming to address race and discrimination especially for their Black employees. I was a year past the divorce; I had rebuilt the garden.

Now, after a decade and more as a Quaker and as a fairly newly ordained Dharma teacher, I looked back. I had navigated so much, and mostly I kept going, moving forward, without pause, largely alone. But what support, what connection is important to me? Who is really there for me? What does it mean to "stop everything"? How much work is enough? How can I stop hoping that if I have the right combination of profile photos or a charmingly hip and interesting bio on the dating apps, I will meet someone, that person who has not yet appeared in my life? What if I don't say yes to every invitation to work? What if I decide to find myself all over again, to rediscover what I am called to do and to be in this season of my life? What if this message, this voice I heard so clearly, is calling me to connect back to me?

I've been so driven by doing: getting out of Brooklyn (before it became hip), passing the bar exam (that was hard), having a successful career (nearly killed off my soul), divorcing with love (letting go of a toxic relationship to heal)—all forces that kept me moving too fast in an already speeding-up world. Too many days had me feeling I was running in place, moving from task to task, accomplishing lots of stuff yet wondering, "Does any of this bring me closer to what is a genuine and authentic expression of this gift of my life?"

A few weeks or maybe days after my voice-at-the-kitchen-sink moment, the storm came. It began as a drizzle, then a trickle, and became a full-blown hurricane with tornado-like wind and rain. Honestly, I didn't see the record-breaking, hundred-year storm called Hurricane Ida coming! It took the East Coast of the United States by surprise and lasted only twenty-four hours. For days afterward, people here told stories about drivers washed away when they tried to cross the sudden tsunami-like force of water—in some cases six feet of water—overflowing creeks and streams, flooding streets, asphalt driveways, and patches of undeveloped land. Some survivors on the road that night clawed their way out of their vehicles and sought the safety of a tree, only to be swept away by gale-force winds and then blown down what had been four-lane highways.

Whatever was happening around me ahead of that storm, I had been busy designing and creating a week of fun for my great-niece and -nephew, Cindy and Jonathan, ages nine and three—trying to give them an unforgettable end-of-summer experience before they returned to their overscheduled routines. I had been consumed by our days spent exploring nearby meadows with late-season grasses, butterflies, and wildflowers, picking blueberries and flowers in a damp drizzle, visiting the Museum of Natural History in New York City, the Crayola Factory in Easton, Pennsylvania, teaching Cindy how to make savory puff pastries and homemade matcha lattes, exploring a life-size castle made for kids and then Henry Chapman Mercer's historic poured-concrete forty-four-room mansion, Fonthill Castle. Finally, after we returned to my home from breakfast at a country café, where we had watched propeller planes take off and land, it was time to send them off with their mom, my niece. I was too tired to fight Philadelphia traffic to take them to the airport and return, so I said my goodbyes and got them a car service. I'm grateful I did. The storm was a monster, washing out roads, capsizing trees, leaving mud and muck in heaps everywhere.

Hurricane Ida brought everything to a hard stop. As I mentioned in the introduction, the hurricane tore through my house, destroying the basement and first floor. My daily routine as I knew it came to a halt as I singly refocused from my work and routines to shoveling and hauling mud out the basement, rebuilding the first floor, and remediating fast-growing mold from the receding water. The storm was like a cosmic message, saying, "Your life needs to shift now."

More than a hurricane, the storm was a wake-up call, a reminder of the ways I'd forgotten what living genuine really means. With the hurricane, I was confronted with my well-developed tendency to go it alone, to be super independent. There was no way for me to handle the damage from the storm alone. The hurricane was a moment of reckoning in the personal, professional, interior, all spheres of my life.

In the Plum Village tradition, we train in two fundamental mindfulness meditation practices: stopping (*shamatha*) and looking deeply (*vipassana*). Stopping isn't just about being still. It's one thing to still the body and another thing to still the mind. To remind myself of the importance of the practice of stopping, I hung outside my window two hammocks: one in colors of the ocean, soft hues of blue and green, and the other bright yellow, red, and green. I look out the window at them but seldom actually use them. There is too much inner restlessness and a well-practiced and unremitting energy that keeps me on the move.

Listening to the inner voice, I understood that lazing in the hammock was an aspiration to make space in my life. This wasn't about stopping because I was ready; it was about stopping because it was the wise thing to do. Listening to the voice, I knew that stopping was about recognizing this bafflingly beautiful and astonishing world. My task continues to be to clear away, to make space to actually live it, be pleasured by it, soak it up in my pores. I know I am being called to practice stopping, and I need lots of practice in how to actually do this. The hammocks are still there, and rather than being an object of aspiration, they've become part of my practice of purposefully slowing down.

In his book *Leadership Dojo*, Richard Strozzi-Heckler speaks of the Rule of 300/3000.[1] He says if you want to get good at something, you need to practice doing it over and over again. To be specific, it takes three hundred repetitions to develop a bodily memory of a skill and three thousand repetitions to fully embody it. Practice builds mastery. Hesitation, procrastination, self-doubt, and anxiety are part of the process toward mastery. It's the effort to practice that transforms over time into embodiment.

Since Hurricane Ida in 2021, I have rededicated myself to practice stopping and looking deeply with the practice of truth telling, which is like surplus beauty. And surplus beauty is like this: You're walking down the street, and a leaf glides from a tree, and you're really there to see it in the moment. Or you're looking up at the sky and feel the floatiness of a cloud. Or someone, a stranger, stops to look at you while holding a door open, and you say, "Thank you," and look at them with a fleeting connection and completeness. These moments I return to over and over again remind me that nothing stays the same. Everything is changing: days, hours, years, seasons, people, desires. And it's up to us to be here now, to bring ourselves back from being either partially or fully checked out to this unrepeatable moment. Truth telling invites us to look squarely into our heart and ask, "What is true now?" And truth telling invites us over and over again.

In truth telling, I see that underneath the losses—the relationships that could have worked out but didn't, the people I loved who are gone—is a sense of half-belonging. I belonged to them, and they are gone. I belonged to a career as a lawyer, and that is gone. I belonged in a marriage, and that is over. I ask myself, "Where do I belong now and with whom?" The need to belong, to be connected, isn't just important, as I wrote in chapter 6, it's a biological imperative. Without it, we cannot survive. It's as necessary as food and water. Yet at times, belonging feels unattainable—in plain sight but just out of reach.

While engaging in the practice of making peace with the longing to belong, embracing the paradox of that longing, I understood it also connected me to everyone who has ever felt abandoned, left behind, disappointed, washed-up, confused, or weary. Rather than the longing creating a wedge that made me an oddball, the longing united me with everybody else reckoning with the scarred places of life. Like everybody else who has ever taken the risk to love, to belong, I, too, was learning, relearning that love and belonging are fragile. They're not meant to be here forever. You hold on to them for a while. You savor them. You release them. If you're lucky, you recognize that love and belonging come back to you in the giveaway—giving it away, no strings attached.

Belonging, like stopping, takes practice, a lot of practice. Understanding the 300/3000 rule, here's how I began after the storm. I told myself, "You invite a new friend out for a walk. You speak up at a work meeting even when you're uncertain. You take yourself out on a date to the movies or to a local park. You attend the local block party even though you don't know anyone." Belonging begets connection, and connection builds authentic relationships.

Belonging requires the practice of listening to others, as well as to ourselves, and embracing inner truth. I acknowledged three big, hard inner truths of my life: First, I don't have a giant collection of friends, true friends, close friends, though I have loads of people who admire and care about me. Hardly a week goes by that I don't receive a card or a letter (yes, some people still have the old-fashioned and thoughtful practice of handwriting notes and cards). When I forget that I am loved, I take out these cards and read them.

Second, I love my work, *and* I am also being drawn from coaching and consulting to writing. I am being called to find myself all over again in new ways—as a writer who coaches and consults, from a coach and consultant who writes—and see what emerges. (Just admitting this truth scares me a little.)

Third, this is a time to practice as never before, stopping everything that doesn't bring me closer to a more genuine and authentic life. What that looks like for me is moment-by-moment truth telling. Today as I move about town, I see three different interracial couples. It's Saturday, and the weather is gorgeous. This triggers loneliness, and I procrastinate going home alone.

Truth telling is being vulnerable enough to admit to myself this hurts *and* to make dinner of baked tofu with green figs and rosemary and sit out on my deck gazing at the black-eyed Susans. I get lucky and a hummingbird darts by. I have a demanding week ahead, and instead of sitting at my desk for hours on a sunny Sunday in late September, I listen to the truth telling within. I take myself out on a date to the beach and place my beach chair right up against the edge of the water, eating the biggest-ever, juicy, end-of-summer peach you've ever seen. That is living the truth. That is practicing it, over and over.

Truth telling is essential to healing ourselves and healing the world. It is about waking up from the social conditioning that keeps us on the hamster wheel of productivity, perfectionism, and performance. It's not that those things aren't important, but through my own life, I've discovered these have been way out of alignment with living authentically.

> *To be brave is to find a different path. Bravery is about not following our conditioning but choosing something else or finding another way.*
>
> —*Annie Lake Mahon*

Truth telling is about not just doing our best but about giving ourselves space. It's not about getting rid of the feelings of loneliness, half-belonging, self-doubt, or isolation but about befriending them. Truth telling acknowledges the hairy monster of striving to succeed, to prove myself, to perform even when conditions beg for ease, cry out for softness, tenderness, and space.

When we begin working with coaching students at the Georgetown University's Leadership Coaching Program, we start in the very first of six modules introducing them to these domains of humanness to support them in becoming open, curious, and flexible to their inner emotions, thoughts, feelings, values, assumptions, and beliefs, so they are better able to access and build deeper understanding of their emotional, physical, spiritual, and mental capabilities for themselves and for the clients they will serve. What they discover is that truth telling is a practice, lived over and over. It requires stopping and listening, and that supports our authenticity and awareness in all domains of the human experience: our body, mind, emotions, soul, and identity.

Body

Most of us these days spend way too much time on screens, sitting. We know this isn't good for the body; we know it's causing us to walk around hunched over, shoulder rounded, head jutting forward. We know that living authentically invites us to listen to our bodies and recognize that the body is designed to move. Awareness of the body is the first foundation of mindfulness. We don't need to have the body of an Olympian. We do need to befriend our body. There are countless options. But begin. Begin slowly. If you're able to walk, start walking. If you're able to swim, do that. If you love to dance, go for it. What is important is to begin slowly and do what you love and what is appropriate for your circumstances, listening to the body. It's hard to listen within, to this inner voice of wisdom, if the body is screaming for attention and care. Paying attention to the body supports paying attention to the inner voice.

Galway Kinnell, in his poem "Saint Francis and the Sow," reminds us that "everything flowers, from within."[2] Living authentically in the body happens not just on the outside, when we shape and tone muscle fibers, but also from the inside through interoception, developing an inner sensitivity, an inner attention to our body. This awareness helps us cultivate a felt sense of the body from the inside out. We begin to know when the body is feeling discomfort, when it needs to move or is calling out for rest. Move your body. Notice your posture and practice aligning, stacking the head over the shoulders, over hips, over knees, over feet, and feel the ground. The following two practices will help you pay attention to the body, to the wisdom it brings.

Yin Yoga Practice

Sit in a comfortable position, lie down, or stand.

Take a few deep breaths, then . . .

Feel the ground.

Relax the tongue.

Soften the face.

Soften the belly.

Receive, feel the in- and the out-breath, allowing the breath to be soft and receptive.

Body Practice with Word or Image

Sit in a comfortable position, lie down, or stand. If you are a visual person, you might consider an image, like an anchor or mountain, that gives you a sense of feeling grounded and stable. If you are more verbally oriented, consider a word to bring with you into this practice to help reconnect you to the present moment when your mind wanders. For example, you could say silently to yourself, "Here, now," when your mind wanders.

To begin, take a few deep breaths, then ...

- Breathe in and feel the cool air come into the body.

- Breathe out and feel the warmth of your body.

- Breathe in, feel the ground. Breathe out, feel your feet on the ground.

- Breathe in and out, and just notice the thoughts as they drift by without getting entangled by them.

- See them as passing clouds, coming and going.

- When a thought becomes distracting, refocus your attention on your grounding visual image or turn to a few simple words that help you to find a sense of inner stability.

Continue this practice for two or three minutes. To conclude, stretch in any way that is comfortable for you.

Mind

More than forty years of mindfulness research establishes the importance of practice, of training the body but also training the mind. Mindfulness meditation is a path of mind and heart, training that not only supports greater clarity, awareness, and focus but also helps us become more compassionate. Too often, popular media underscores the attentional component of mindfulness, forgetting its ethical underpinning—that mindfulness helps us become a more openhearted version of ourselves.

Sometimes we can get attached to or stuck on practicing meditation to achieve enlightenment or some other goal. Mindfulness is deeper than striving for goals, even great goals. Instead, a foundational element of mindfulness is nonjudgmental awareness. We reframe our stance to one of openness and curiosity, non-attachment, non-clinging even to a goal.

Decades of research make clear that the brain is malleable, and that we can change even ingrained, conditioned patterns, ways of thinking with practice. (Think 300/3000 rule.) With practice and training, we can notice when we are lost in narrative, worry, rumination, obsessed with goals, or lost in mind-wandering. We are invited to practice stopping, shifting to being here for whatever our experience is in the present.

Thich Nhat Hanh practiced and taught the art of mindful meditation for more than sixty years, wrote more than one hundred books, and offered countless talks. Yet his teachings always contain a basic message: through mindfulness and concentration, we can deepen insight. We can calm the mind and the body. Here is a starting mind practice. Chapter 8 will offer additional practices and queries that build on it.

Awareness of Thoughts Practice

Sit in a comfortable position, lie down, or stand. Take a few deep breaths, then . . .

- Become aware of your breath and body.

- Allow the eyes to close if that is comfortable for you.

- Become aware of your thoughts.

- Notice the nature and quality of your thoughts, your thinking.

- Mentally, give each thought a label, like "worried," "distracted," "calm," or "content." (Mentally noting thoughts helps us to be less attached and more objective about them.)

- Allow the thought to be there as you notice the passing nature of the thought or thought pattern.

- Continue this practice of noticing thoughts and labeling them for two to three minutes.

- Return your awareness to your breath.

- Feel the in- and out-breath.

- Stretch and, if your eyes are closed, open them.

With this and the other mindfulness practices, remember the introduction's guidance for engaging this book: "One Size Doesn't Fit Everyone: Meditation Is Person and Context Specific."

Awareness of Emotions

As practitioners of the Plum Village tradition, we train ourselves in honing skills to handle emotions, particularly strong emotions. Again, this is a practice of not suppressing or denying afflictive emotions like hate, envy, greed, or jealousy. Instead, our practice is to take good care of them, to invite them in for a cup of tea, to get to know them, the root of these emotions, to develop understanding that can help us be with these emotions. Handling emotions, especially strong emotions, requires that we engage our breathing, a conscious and intentional way to build concentration, awareness, and insight. The breath is a barometer of our emotional state. When we're stressed, this is reflected in the breath. When we're feeling calm, the breath gives us feedback about this too. This is insight to the state of our being. With this insight, we have greater capacity to know how to handle our emotions.

Among the emotions I am working with now is my discomfort with and tendency to deflect sincere and genuine compliments. At times, I feel it's hard for me to take in encouragement. As I've said earlier in this book, I also have had difficulty sharing my needs and allowing others to support me (though I'm a lot better at this now). Sometimes I think it's immodest to accept praise. But most of the time, this goes back to an old story that I am undeserving of true affection. When I was growing up, affection was in short supply. It was there for sure, yet it had to be earned, mostly through hard work. I came to believe I had to perform really, really well to earn love. So I detached myself from the need for love and became super self-sufficient. Obviously, this old story backfired. The new story is this: With every breath I take, I know love is there. In every relationship, love is there. Love begins with me, with choosing love, no matter what.

Emotions Practice: "Choose Love" Affirmation

Hope and bravery are habits that are asking me not only to love well but also to discover what loves me back. Lately, the following affirmation has taken up space in my heart. Try it. Repeat this silently to yourself:

> *No matter what, I choose love.*
> *Say it with conviction.*
> *Say it in the voice of a whisper.*
> *Say it before you go to sleep at night, and then say it the first thing when you wake up in the morning.*
> *Say it over and over again to yourself until the affirmation is etched in your heart.*

Awareness of Identity

At first glance, it seems obvious that we would know ourselves pretty well by a certain age, that we would know the fullness of our identity. Yet it's actually hard to do. It requires truth telling, self-reflection—things we don't do enough. When parts of ourselves are challenging, we don't confront them. Or those aspects of ourselves that may be hidden from us, aspects that are not apparent, we don't reflect on. For the blind spots we might encounter within, nature has beautiful metaphors when we engage self-awareness to begin to unearth our identity: a flower opening slowly; an iceberg, where we can see what is above the waterline and know that much more is below the waterline; tree roots, which spread far beyond a tree's canopy; or an onion, where we can peel back its layers gradually.

As a Black woman, I understand identity as fundamental to personhood. By identity, I also mean intersectionality, vulnerability, and complexity—all parts of us. Yet there is so much more. Each of us is assigned at birth by our society a social group identity because of our shared characteristics. These characteristics are with the dominant culture, which holds power and controls societal norms, rewards, and values, or the nondominant culture, which doesn't. Social group identity is based on many categories that locate us in society, such as ethnicity, religion, sexual orientation, and language.

As a Black lawyer, I hold a nondominant social group identity by virtue of my race, and as a lawyer, I hold a dominant social group identity by virtue of my education, training, and experience. Many people in this field of research say for Black people in particular and people of color in general, our social group identity affiliated with race trumps any dominant identity we might hold, such as college education or being cisgender, because of the effects of systemic and structural racism, structural discrimination, concentrated poverty, and socioeconomic disparities that perpetuate inequity.

As a Black person, I am called to deepen my self-awareness of my social group identity and the ways I am subject to cultural conditioning. We can internalize a sense of inferiority and powerlessness. This can become racialized trauma and internalized racial oppression. White people can internalize a sense of superiority that then becomes white supremacist thinking. As a Black woman, I had a deep wounding of internalized oppression even though I attended a historically Black law school and despite all my achievements. This inferiority was fueled by exhaustion from racial discrimination, as I constantly tried to prove myself.

It's important to recognize how we have been socially and culturally conditioned because of our social group identity to recognize where we hold power and to recognize that we hold both dominant and nondominant social group identities. Understanding our identity means understanding ourselves. Truth telling grounds our identity and becomes grounded in our identity. To live our most genuine self begins with knowing and speaking from the depth of who we are. As we do, our work in the world is then connected to who we are and what we value.

IDENTITY-SHAPING REFLECTION AND PRACTICE

Time: 15–30 minutes
Participants: 3

Gather two people to engage this reflective practice. Then take five minutes of quiet time to journal or jot a note about what has shaped your identity. Who are the people and what are the places and events that have shaped your life? With your small group, have a conversation about your responses and what you've discovered about identity, using the community agreements or discussion guidelines provided in chapter 6.

Awareness of Spirit/Soul

A powerful metaphor for the spirit or soul element of living a genuine and authentic life sits on my desk: *matryoshka* dolls, sometimes called Russian nesting dolls. They speak of the ever-deepening quality of spiritual and soulful awakening, of layers revealed. To explore spirit is to risk those layers becoming visible: there is always a part of the inner journey we are not fully awake to or aware of.

Another way to think about exploring the spirit is to imagine driving on an unknown road, lost. You don't get down on yourself; instead, you get out your navigation device and get back on track, you practice self-forgiveness, self-regard, self-compassion—even as you discover unknown roads. This reality of spirit invites us into a moment when we might touch a little sadness, a knowing that there is a part of us that others may never know, that we cannot share with anyone because it is also elusive to us.

Even so, there are countless ways to touch the soul. Throughout this book, I have shared many of them: through risking love, risking hope, risking courage, we touch, recognize, and build the soul, one moment at a time, one practice after another. When we live a soul-centered life, our values, actions, even our checkbook (to use an old-fashioned term) align. A soul-centered life may not always feel good, but it always feels *real*. We reach out and keep reaching out with our uncertainty, our ambiguity, and our unresolved longing. And when we offer acceptance of that which is hidden within us, of our longing, this is like a seed in the wind that finds a fertile place to take hold. Risking your heart, risking again and again to love, reveals the soul.

We cannot lead, or write, or pray, or teach, or make love from a place of exhaustion or defending against the pain and loss that life will ultimately throw our way. We have to fill ourselves up first, drink from our own well, rest in a hammock, nourish ourselves as we take great risk and great care. This is where the soul's hiddenness becomes less hidden. And this is the kind of soul understanding that leads to liberation, to creating an authentic self and an authentic life.

* * *

When I am stressed from uncertainty and anxiety, filled with wanting to manage and shape the day as I have shaped much of my life through directness, assertiveness, and control, I remember to look instead for the place of soul nourishment.

I return to my garden and to my hammock. Maybe I look out the window or, better still, step outside and place my feet on a patch of grass and look up at the twenty-foot-high, frosty-celadon green *Hydrangea paniculata*, 'Limelight;' the true-blue *Agastache foeniculum* covered with honeybees; and the gold-flowering *Rudbeckia hirta*. I get a whiff of the earth, this reality, knowing where my feet are planted, touching the earth.

As I take in the garden, I also take in the sounds and smells around me, and I can, even for a few moments, surrender my willpower and assertiveness to the soft grass under my feet. I feel nourished by this moment.

I think back to the day when I was standing at the kitchen sink and heard my inner voice of wisdom say, "Stop everything. Stop." I embraced and continued to listen to this inner voice. Though it was scary at first and I was uncertain, I no longer have any doubt. The voice of the soul, the inner truth-telling voice, and the genuine vulnerability and courage developed through the practices described in this book bring me home, back to what is vitally real and meaningful in my life. And "real" and "meaningful" are a very good place to be.

SEVEN FACTORS OF AWAKENING: THE SEVENTH FACTOR, EQUANIMITY

Most of us are thrown off balance at some point, and we need *upekkha*, sometimes translated as "nondiscrimination," to bring us back to equanimity. Even when overtaken by loss or gain, we can return to a state of nondiscrimination. With the global pandemic, this has been a tall order. A modern-day adaptation of equanimity is the quality of resilience, the ability to navigate adversity, to grow and thrive in the face of challenge. To practice equanimity is to reorient toward our strengths and find what supports us. It is about attending to painful life events and reshaping our stories of loss into stories of meaning. It is about moving from what bad thing happened to you to who you choose to become because of it.

To practice navigating the painful moments of life and transform them into moments of recognizing our common humanity is the practice of equanimity. Sometimes that is more than enough.

Real Voices, Real Courage

In 2021, I joined a group of African Americans exploring their dreams, using Jungian frameworks under the leadership of Jungian analyst Dr. Fanny Brewster. Long before I joined the group, I was drawn to Brewster's truth telling, especially through her interpretation of dreams. Her clarity about the meaning and symbols of dreams caused me to stop and look deeply at what my dreams were revealing to me.

Recently, she sat down with me to talk about her life, work, hope, and bravery. Here's what she said.

Fanny Brewster

She/her

Jungian analyst, writer, lecturer on creativity, dreamwork, and spirituality

"You have to begin with understanding that you're not born with courage. Courage develops, bravery develops, because you encounter things that work that muscle; otherwise, you don't know where you stand. I think being able to take a position and knowing where you stand in your life psychologically is a part of understanding your cowardice and understanding your bravery."

I was born in a small town, south of Myrtle Beach, South Carolina. I was raised in a home that belonged to my grandmother until my father built a home for us. My grandmother was also my midwife, so she brought me into the world. It was an auspicious and wonderful beginning, having my grandmother be my midwife. I stayed in that town until I was eleven years old, and then my family moved to New York City, to Brooklyn.

My father's mother—my paternal grandmother—was influential. I would spend time with her while my parents went to work. My father's sister was away in Detroit, and my mother's sister could have taken care of me, but of course, it fell to my grandmother instead, so she and I were really close. On Sundays I went with my grandmother to church. I would sit on her front porch with her, swinging as people passed by, calling, "Hi, Miss Becca!" to greet her and stopping by the fence to talk in that very southern way. I have her middle name, Rebecca.

I was drawn to dreamwork quite young. I would talk to my grandmother about my dreams. Back then, I had what I now call archetypal dreams. Looking back at them, they seemed scary and magnificent and something I couldn't even imagine. I was a kid—ten years old, nine years old—and was having these amazing dreams in my childhood. Then as the years went by, I kept dream journals.

I began an early career as a speech-language pathologist. However, one day, I was talking to a colleague, and I said, "I really wish I could do more with my dreams." I had been studying dreamwork with a colleague who was a dream worker and teacher. He began a school in Berkeley for studying dreams, and I attended that school for a time, lived in Berkeley, and felt drawn to become more immersed in studying dreams.

Eventually, I found my way to Pacifica Graduate Institute and began studying dreams and doing dream-work in its school of depth psychology. I completed my studies at Pacifica and then started working on my dissertation in New York. At that point, I decided I could do more by becoming a Jungian analyst. Basically, I came to be a Jungian analyst through the backdoor because I don't think I ever said, "I want to be a Jungian analyst." Honestly, that is a professional label, but it's not my primary label. My interest was always in dreamwork.

Dreams can teach us about bravery. They are significant for who we are, who we were, and who we are evolving into. Dreams help shape the personality, and a part of one's personality is about learning how to be courageous.

Many years ago, when I studied with Helen Palmer, a pioneer in the development of the study of the Enneagram, I discovered what my point was on the Enneagram: being a six is that ego-coward place. The Enneagram contains points of ego reference. It also indicates a place of higher consciousness, a place of spirituality. The indication of an ego-point helps bring understanding to areas of potential psychological growth. For me, delving into knowing more about the characteristics of this ego-reference allowed me to see those places where I was conditioned to be afraid, really afraid, of living my own life.

Through the Enneagram and my work with Helen Palmer, I have learned that you have to start with knowing the things you're afraid of. You have to begin with understanding that you're not born with courage. Courage develops, bravery develops, because you encounter things that work that muscle; otherwise, you don't know where you stand. I think being able to take a position and knowing where you stand in your life psychologically is a part of understanding your cowardice and understanding your bravery.

Who's brave every moment? No one is brave every single moment. We have to choose our battles, choose when we're going to walk away. It's not cowardice. It's just being able to say, "This is not a battle I can win," and be able to walk away from it. Understanding bravery and cowardice is deeply psychological. What does it really mean to be a coward? Sometimes it looks like cowardice. And sometimes it looks like you're just making the best choice that you can, given the circumstances.

When you look at dreams, you're looking at the ego personality, and you're also looking at all of the unconscious material that's alive in those dreams. You can look at a dream and determine what the mother complex is, what the father complex is that's being activated in the wake state. For example, you can see how someone is running in their dream. What are they running to—or from? What is the level of anxiety or confidence or courage that they're feeling as they're running? Sometimes they're dreaming about fighting and engagement or about anxiety and feeling that they're losing the struggle. So what does that bring up, and what does that say about one's bravery and courage? And then sometimes in a dream, a person can have a fight and feel victorious in the moment, and then the ego is strengthened. The ego becomes strengthened because there's energy and power in the unconscious, so that energy becomes charged, and the person feels victorious and wakes up feeling fabulous.

Our dream state often depends on how we wake up. We wake up in the morning feeling sad, or we feel discouraged, or we feel courageous, or we feel good. We may not even remember the dream, but our emotional state might be because of something that happened in the dream. So in being able to look at one's dream and look at the ego in the dream, you're able to ascertain what is called the shadow: things of the life hidden in the unconscious that the ego fails to see. In Jungian language, you're able to look at that shadow and say, "Oh, this is the weakness in my personality. I turned away. I was a coward in that moment," or "I turned away, and that was the better thing to have done."

Dreams show us so much about our ability to be courageous—our ability to face our fears. They teach us how we can show up in all of our potential. As people of color, we are always experiencing vulnerability. We are discriminated against in every way possible; we are killed, we are murdered. And yes, we have to be able to be vulnerable within ourselves. Otherwise, we become like stone; we become like rock.

Vulnerability is a fluid motion because it's not always an action. It can take many forms. For example, vulnerability can be like still water. There is vulnerability in being silent, and there is vulnerability in listening. Most importantly, for a person of color, vulnerability is learning how to move from a marginal place into the center and to determine that one has the ability to move there. We need to understand the weaknesses in the personality to be able to draw on strength and resilience.

I'll share an important moment that was both vulnerable and courageous. I had studied at the University of San Francisco for a degree in speech-language pathology. I had done all the coursework for this degree, and I had taken the national licensing test but failed because I wasn't a good test taker. I took it the second time and passed. I completed my master's degree and applied for my license after doing a huge amount of work, which took years. When I applied for the license, I was denied because I was three-quarters of a unit short to fulfill my academic requirements.

I was really angry because I felt the licensing board was being petty and rigid. There was no flexibility at all. I actually had the units, three of them, but the board was refusing to accept even three-quarters of one unit from the three that I had on my undergraduate transcript. I went back through all my undergraduate and graduate transcripts and hired a lawyer to appeal my case. During the board meeting, the lawyer was sitting there, not saying anything, and these board members—five or six of them—were really pushing him around. I turned to my lawyer and said, "Let me talk for myself here. Let me just say what I need to say." I started talking, and the board reversed its decision. I did receive my license; I won my case. That was a defining moment for me.

There's something about being able to constantly expand one's horizon through self-reflection, to be imaginal about oneself, and to be able to, in a moment, move in different ways that allow you to step into whom you need to be, like stepping into your bravery, stepping into your own vulnerability. These all must be claimed by you, not anyone else.

MINDFULNESS PRACTICE: TOUCHING THE EARTH

Time Required: 5 minutes or more

As was stated in the introduction, meditation is not one-size-fits-all. Consider your circumstance, access, ability, and needs and adapt the practice accordingly. For example if balance is a concern, consider sitting or lying down. If access to the outdoors is not available to you, consider gazing out a window.

The Plum Village community has a practice of being in touch with the earth, of surrendering our difficulties to the earth, to allow the earth herself to absorb our pain. The earth is forgiving, renewable, and sustaining, and when we practice remembering that we are made of the earth, and really connecting with the earth, we can feel a sense of relief and ease.

Here's an adaptation of the Plum Village practice that can be done in any outdoor space:

- Step outside.

- Allow your senses to take in the moment.

- Allow an inner quiet to settle into your body and mind for a few breaths.

- Feel the ground beneath your feet.

- Imagine surrendering concerns, worries, frustrations to the ground.

- Notice and feel the stability of the ground and allow that to support you.

- Notice how you feel.

- When you are ready, stretch gently.

QUERIES

The Quaker practice of the clearness committee is spiritual discernment in community.[3] The foundation for the clearness committee is the belief among Friends that every person has access to Inner Wisdom, inner guidance, and their Inner Teacher, and therefore there is no need for problem solving or fixing. That basic stance is highly countercultural in our fix-it, problem-solving culture. But when we approach others with the confidence and trust that they already have access to this Inner Wisdom as a gift from God and that our role is to be part of a supportive and loving community to bear witness to this Inner Wisdom, we are truly free.

The next time you are with a friend who is struggling over vexing concerns, rather than offering solutions or giving unsolicited advice, instead offer your friend your undivided presence and an open question, such as one of these:

- What have you learned about yourself?

- What have you learned about this concern you are holding?

- If you thought differently, how would this change things for you?

Chapter 8

BRAVELY HOME: BOUNDLESS JOY (WELL, MAYBE BASIC OKAYNESS) ON THE WAY BACK TO YOU

There are ways in, journeys to the center of a life, through time, through air, matter, dream, and thought. The ways in are not always mapped or charted, but sometimes being lost, if there is such a thing, is the sweetest place to be. And always, in this search, a person might find that she is already there, at the center of a world. It may be a broken world, but it is glorious nevertheless.

—*Linda Hogan*[1]

This final chapter is a beginning, not an ending. It continues my life chapters and yours. I began this book with the image of wayfarers of ancient times on the open seas using navigational devices—the map, guide, compass, or sextant—but those old tools can't take us in a new direction. We, too, are wayfarers courageously leaning toward hope, toward a new location and direction, toward the soul, the True Self, to our longing and belonging, toward home.

When I first started this book, I was heartbroken from the end of my fifteen-year marriage. Today, almost two years later, I am broken open and clear that the divorce was a necessary ending to create a necessary beginning full of hope, courage, and much possibility. What I discovered in this time were practices and shifts in mindset and heartset, in my soul, that helped me. My hope is that if I share them with you, they will help bring you back to you, maybe better. There are no guarantees. This is the inner work of hope and courage. It's not easy, but it is worth the effort.

To live bravely in a beautiful and broken world requires that you see clearly. Take off the blinders. Stop running. Stop wishing for things to be other than what they are. Accept this present moment as it is, not reminiscing about the past or fast-forwarding into a yet-to-be-determined future, but instead firmly grounded in *now*. From this grounding and connectedness, you can explore your values, beliefs, assumptions, and assessments. You can begin to rewrite the story of your life. You can move bravely toward a home within yourself.

Hope, like happiness, as you know, isn't a constant. It isn't a place where we set up camp and live forever. Hope, like happiness, courage, and bravery, is a choice. It doesn't necessarily track what's happening to our daily life or the external world around us. It is not predictable or constant. Hope isn't like a degree you hang on the wall and admire. Instead, it's more like Play-Doh, the kids' clay-like toy that you smush, squeeze, and mold into shapes. Hope is malleable.

That molding requires our creative work. And to create a life where hope leans forward, we need to have at least three things being shaped in us:

- Joy, or a sense of your own basic okayness

- Belonging to you

- Courage to live your purpose

In this chapter, we'll focus on each of these.

Joy, or a Sense of Basic Okayness

Recently I had one of those unimaginably beautiful days when the world appears whitewashed, almost glittery. Light was everywhere, rising and falling on green leaves, settling high in the September sky, flowing over people and sidewalks, illuminating everything it touched. On days like this, my vision takes in everything, and everyone is my best friend. I forget plans and schedules. I saw the day itself as too important a gift to be boxed in by an agenda, so I said yes to the day.

These moments are experiences but also the continuing of practices, like beginning the day with yoga classes where I can still feel an opening and stretchiness in my legs and lower back. "I'm glad to be alive," I think, "on this day in particular but also meeting each day." At yoga class, I've learned that unless I am attentive, I can make a yoga class into a competition. I can get into a mindset of pushing and striving that leaves me with a sense of inner struggle. But on this glittery day, I left class feeling alive to my breath, my body.

It wasn't always like that. When I began studying Kundalini yoga decades ago, as I wrote earlier, I was muscular and stiff as a board. I couldn't bend forward without low-back pain, and I thought exercise meant working out the parts of the body that are most visible, like the biceps. I thought that "progress" in yoga, like my legal career, meant striving, muscling your way through. If I wasn't in pain, I must be doing it wrong. I was so accustomed to the mindset of struggle, pushing hard, pushing through with grit.

As I began to practice the balance postures, they taught me I needed to yield and not demand, to release, and most importantly, to soften. I recall the moment things began to change. I was attending a weekend Kundalini yoga retreat at a rustic stone and timber retreat center in the Poconos Mountains. Our practice began at the Amrit Vela. In the Kundalini yoga tradition, this is the start of a new day among many Sikhs, beginning at roughly three to six in the morning. The "sweet nectar," as it is called, is a time to practice meditation, a time when energetically we are most open.

I was feeling the softness of the day just beginning, rose-colored light pouring into the center of the circular room and the sun rising above the mountains out of the darkness. Our back-bending and heart-opening *kriyas*, or yoga postures, left me feeling unguarded and less defended by the time we closed the session with *savasana*, or corpse posture, lying flat on the floor with arms and legs spread comfortably apart, eyes closed, breathing, doing nothing.

I felt my heart wide and open. *Savasana* engages the parasympathetic nervous system; it calms and soothes. It is a posture of integration and consolidation, a moment to feel changed from the internal effects of the yoga practice from the inside out. And it is also said to be one of the hardest postures in yoga, though it looks easy. The challenge with this posture is to quiet and settle the mind as the body is in stillness. The moment I went into this posture, my thoughts rambled something like this: "I really need to work on opening my hips. I'll go for a walk before breakfast. I should have brought the other blanket." And so on. As the thoughts continued, gradually I turned my attention away from thinking to noticing the weight of my body on the floor, my heels touching the mat, and the place where the back of my head met the mat. I felt the center of my chest, my heart. I was alive. I was okay. My heart opened. From the outside, I realized, the yoga pose didn't show what was happening. But yoga is about what you feel on the inside. And at that moment, I felt alive.

Breaking Free from Negative Thinking

While the moments of feeling totally alive and openhearted come—sometimes as a surprise—that internal sense of freedom or even basic okayness can feel illusive. When my thoughts are on autopilot and self-focused, my thinking tends to wander into patterns dredged up from the past. That wandering mind is a cause of unhappiness, Daniel Goleman says in his book *Focus: The Hidden Driver of Excellence.*[2] When our thinking turns self-focused, this "me" thinking links to the default mode of the mind, perpetuating a restless, wandering stream of thoughts, leading to additional thoughts that enlarge the belief of not-okayness. This mental mode is activated when the mind is in passive focus. That's where practice comes in. When we're in active focus, such as mindfully breathing or moving through a yoga sequence, the brain turns off the self-referential focus.

To break free from this pattern of reinforcing a wandering mind and negative thinking, I like to use a four-step process:

1. Notice the thoughts.
2. Name the thoughts.
3. Reframe thinking.
4. Repeat for the rest of your life.

The first step is to notice your thinking. Notice the nature and quality of your thinking and how you are feeling. This is similar to, and builds on, the mindfulness practice in chapter 7. Is there a connection between what you're thinking and how you're feeling? How would you categorize your thoughts? Are they repetitive? Are they thoughts about the past? Are they fantasy about the future? Is there a connection between your thinking, feelings, and emotions? Is there a connection between your emotions and your actions? If so, what emotions are present for you when you are lost in me-centered, ruminating thoughts? What actions result from this emotional state?

The ability to notice when I'm lost in negative, me-centered thinking and to reframe is a powerful skill and the beginning of actively cultivating joy, which doesn't necessarily need to mean that everything is fabulous one hundred percent of the time. Joy is about feeling well-being with the circumstances of your life in the moment. It doesn't mean there isn't room for improvement or you don't have desires. It does mean that you accept who you are, knowing that this is always changing.

The second step is to name your thinking. Once you've noticed that you are thinking and you've noticed the nature of your thinking, meaning you are aware your thinking is self-directed, persistent, and not supporting you, it's up to you to do something about it. Naming has power. Naming what's happening takes you out of the mindless loop of second-guessing and ruminating and into being more objective, less attached and overidentified with your own thinking.

In their book *The Practice of Adaptive Leadership: Tools and Tactics for Changing Your Organization and the World*, Ronald Heifetz, Alexander Grashow, and Marty Linsky say that in a complex and constantly changing world, it's important to metaphorically "get on the balcony," that is, to move outside or above your repetitive thinking to gain a clearer view of the bigger picture from another perspective.[3] They encourage readers to move away from a conflict or challenge to get a wider perspective and to ask, "What is going on here?" As I wrote in chapter 6, as a student of Thich Nhat Hanh, I have daily experienced and lived his important question: "Are you sure?" Questions like these begin to unlock and open up what can be very mechanical thinking. These questions bring you back to a basic sense that you are okay and may need to hit the reset button on your thinking. Nothing is fundamentally wrong with you.

The third step—after you have noticed negative thinking and named it and have been able to get on the "balcony" of your own mind and move away from the conveyer belt of negative, ruminating thoughts—is to reframe your thinking. Ask yourself, "Is this true? Is there another way to look at this?" Refocus your thoughts on the positive in your life. Create a new thought that is supportive. Replace the negative, degenerating thought with a regenerating thought. Focus on what makes you feel hopeful and joyful. Shift from what is wrong to what is right with you and with this moment.

The fourth step is to keep doing this for the rest of your life. Like breathing, this is an essential and lifelong practice. You don't master this in a single try or even dozens of attempts. Instead, you practice over and over again. (Recall the 300/3000 rule from chapter 7.) With time, you begin to catch moments when you're spiraling toward a negative mental abyss. You stand up for yourself because you're on your own side. You belong to you, and you love, care, and respect yourself. You make a new and different choice toward a new story in a new moment that supports you. An open, undefended heart and the experience of joy aren't some abstract experience "out there." The experience is inside, and like that glittery, sparkly

September day, shines brightly from the inside out. Our life's work is to let it shine.

Belonging to You: Becoming Beach Glass

As I wrote earlier, I grew up in a Caribbean family of people who did their best to assimilate in the United States. That was tricky. They adopted not only the best of American culture and values but also some of the worst. Growing up, I was pulled between at least two cultures, American culture on the one hand and Caribbean culture—specifically, Cuban and Jamaican cultures—on the other. Often, when I felt the pulling, I asked myself, "Where do I belong?" In school, to belong, I became the shy, quiet one. In my work life, belonging meant fitting in with the white dominant structure of the legal profession. At best, this was confusing and brutal for my self-regard and self-worth.

In recent years, I've asked myself these questions: *What community can I call my own? Who are the folks who have my back? Where do I fit in?* These questions dug deep into years and years of programming that sometimes pointed to a painful answer: *I don't belong.* In the work and practice of rewiring the synapse in my brain toward a different answer, I am answering with a more loving, more generative, less judgy story.

* * *

I love walking along the ocean coastline, and sometimes I'm surprised, delighted really, to find tiny pieces of sea glass or beach glass—broken bits of bottles and other broken glass that have been rolled and tumbled in the ocean for years until all the sharp edges are rounded off and the slickness of the glass has been worn to a frosted appearance. The glass is a beautiful metaphor for transformation. Like the glass shaped by tides, waves, sun, sand, currents, day and night, rain and wind, and so much more, we, too, are shaped into belonging by many forces.

As with the yogic practice of *savasana*, at least part of the work of belonging is belonging to yourself, consolidating and integrating wholeheartedness, smoothing the rough edges, softening the shards into a polished pebble of the heart. I belong. You belong, and that begins with belonging to yourself. It turns out that this sense of belonging is a hidden factor not only for a life of hope and courage, a life well lived, but also for your health. About an hour's drive from my home is the town of Roseto, Pennsylvania, and the people there are a remarkable example of the critical link between belonging and well-being. In the 1950s and 1960s, most residents of Roseto were working-class Italian immigrants from the same small town in Italy. Many were overweight, consuming a diet high in saturated fats and leading sedentary lifestyles. They lived and worked in the Slate Belt in the quarries, surrounded by environmental pollutants.

You would expect that in a place like Roseto, with such lifestyles and environmental conditions, people would die early. Surprisingly, researchers found just the opposite, describing what is now known as the Roseto effect: the phenomenon by which a close-knit community with strong social ties, many social connections, and a sense of belonging is associated with better health, particularly lower rates of heart disease. In Roseto, unlike the neighboring towns, people often lived in multigenerational households. They would stop to talk to neighbors sitting on their front porches. Toddlers played with grandparents. In Roseto in the early 1960s, the crime rate was nearly zero. The community was permeated with a strong sense of belonging and trust. Interestingly, a thirty-year follow-up study showed that heart attack rates gradually rose to match those of neighboring towns, but it wasn't until 1971 that the first person under the age of forty-five died from a heart attack.[4]

Belonging matters. This is something the people of Roseto lived into. I would add to that lesson this thought: Belonging begins with you. To belong to community and with others, we must first belong to ourselves. Accept yourself. Find yourself. Be kind to yourself, and then find others to share the feeling.

You belong to you. Like ocean glass, you are formed by the world around you. You belong to the community of humans, plants, and animals that share this planet. Allow everything that comes your way, like the wind and waves that shape glass to a frosted, polished surface, to shape and reshape your heart until you become a fuller, richer, more alive expression of you. Sit yourself down. Look yourself in the eye (metaphorically speaking). Recall the ancestors who are with you even now. Let yourself belong to you. Then share that with others. Share that with the world. You will discover in those belongings you are practicing living wholeheartedly.

Courage to Live Your Purpose

I've been absolutely terrified every moment of my life— and I've never let it keep me from doing a single thing I wanted to do.

—*Georgia O'Keeffe*

There's a now-famous black-and-white photograph taken in 1944 by Maria Chabot in Abiquiu, New Mexico, of the iconic American painter Georgia O'Keeffe on the back of motorcycle with her friend the painter Maurice Grosser. In the photo, O'Keeffe turns to look at the photographer (as though to the viewer, at us) with a joyful, fearless, knowing grin. O'Keeffe was one of the most significant and intriguing American artists of the twentieth century, known internationally for her boldly innovative art. Her distinct flowers, dramatic cityscapes, glowing landscapes, and images of bones against the stark desert sky are iconic and original contributions to American modernism.

While surely O'Keeffe led a life characterized by great privilege as a white, English-speaking, heterosexual, midwestern, middle-class person, she also, like us all, had struggles. And despite her struggles, she never lost sight of her greater purpose to create through her art an expression of the world. O'Keeffe was a woman who lived her purpose.

Many of us, especially in upwardly mobile, middle-class, heteronormative America, have inherited a mental road map of how life is "supposed" to be. It is some variation of the following: Go to college. Meet someone. Fall in love. Get married. Buy a house. Have a couple of kids. Grow old. Die. For those who are about living your purpose, though, the first step is to begin to question that road map, something many of us have opportunity to do. Many people around the world, because of the conditions of their lives, their environment—living in places beset by climate devastation, war, poverty, displacement, hunger, political instability— have severe limitations on their ability to create new road maps. They struggle under illegal occupation, malnutrition, violence, and more. Yet even in their struggles, profound purpose arises to carry people into new lands, to seek a better life of dignity and basic human rights, to protest political instability, to seek justice, to fight climate devastation, to demand a hopeful future for their children, and to seek justice that goes beyond one's individual circumstance. And there are countless examples of people who have done this, such as Nobel laureates Albert Luthuli, Malala Yousafzai, Maria Ressa, and Dmitry Murato.

Human purpose is what Anthony Burrow studies in his research at Cornell University's College of Human Ecology. He examines why having life direction is so important to a life well lived and how purpose is protective against stress and disease even as it builds resilience. Purpose, says Burrow, can be as simple as meaningful life direction or as complex as a framework for understanding your behaviors, beliefs, and goals[5]. Purpose guides our goals, not the other way around.

Many of us confuse goal-setting with life purpose. Having a sense of purpose contributes meaning to life, and meaning is about what matters most to you. It guides the direction of your life, which changes over time. Living purposefully is living your values—to reflect, understand, and align your values with your action. That's called integrity, and this goes back to what Joan Halifax described as wise hope in the introduction. For those who have economic opportunity, including career choices, and for those who have lost everything, who are seeking to cross borders in search of safety, purpose—a sense of human dignity and meaning—guides those choices.

For many of us, this process of introspection comes at thresholds or times of transition: when closing a year and beginning another or when facing a big life decision, transition, loss, or life-threatening illness. These times invite—and sometimes demand—that we become clear, become brave about what really matters and why. In her poem "The Inside Door," the poet Jan Richardson describes purpose as a door "that opens to the inside"[6]. To live with purpose invites you to reflect on the big, bold questions of your life:

- What is most meaningful to me and why?

- What are my deepest values?

- How do I align my words with my actions?

> *We are called to achieve personhood—to contribute most to others by becoming who we are, and standing for values that matter in this world, whatever the obstacles history provides us.*
>
> —*James Hollis*[7]

> *Meaning is an organ of the soul.*
>
> —James Hollis[8]

Living with purpose is not just about the work you do but also about why you do it. It is about learning about yourself, what you care about, and then doing that. When you discover your purpose, the world is brighter because of it. You bravely return home to you. Howard Thurman famously said, "Don't ask yourself what the world needs. Ask yourself what makes you come alive, and go do that, because what the world needs is people who have come alive." Consider what brings you alive. Consider why. Make this aliveness visible for all to see and feel. This is living courageously, with hope, living with purpose.

Real Voices, Real Courage

In 2020, I began working with a Jewish family foundation, guiding Jewish leaders toward more authentic, compassionate, and trustworthy lives. I met Ilana Kaufman, an extraordinary Black leader in the Jewish community, and was immediately taken with Ilana's joy, sense of aliveness, and clear, bold courage to live purposefully. Here's what Ilana said.

Ilana Kaufman

She/her

Executive Director, Jews of Color Initiative

Avocation: Creating an equitable Jewish community

"Courage and hope give us new openings. They create new opportunities. Courage, bravery, and heart require us to engage in multiple levels and multiple ways, which is exactly how we're designed to engage."

In my professional life, I am the executive director of an organization called the Jews of Color Initiative. Our organization works within the Jewish communal ecosystem in the United States, at the intersection of ecosystemic change and transformation, racial justice, equity, Jews of color, and philanthropy.

I was born and raised in San Francisco, California, which has everything to do with everything in the sense that I was born in 1972. That puts it in a context of a post-Vietnam, Black power, Barbary Coast kind of vibe. I grew up in the Western Addition of San Francisco; white people thought that those of us who were there were living in the projects. The neighborhood and community were filled with African Americans, Jewish people, and the Japanese people who had just been freed from internment camps. It was like the sunniest neighborhood in San Francisco and a great community to grow up in.

I grew up in a housing co-op on the edge of the projects. Everything was about Black power, the end of Freedom Summer, and being raised in a historically rich community that still has a pretty strong Jewish identity in some ways. This really shaped my identity. My mom is white Ashkenazi Jewish from upstate New York. My father is African American Baptist from southeast Texas—Texas City, Texas. I was raised with both families in my life, living primarily in San Francisco but spending the holidays and summers in Texas.

My mom raised me predominantly, not my father, but again, I spent a lot of time with his family. So the story goes that when my twin and I were seven years old, my mother called my grandmother—my father's mother—and said, "You should know you have grandbabies, and I want to raise them Jewish." My mom was raised Modern Orthodox, so what other worldview would she bring to raising her children? At the time, I don't know how she thought about the fact that we were Black—that it was all going to be complicated. But the story goes that my mom called my grandmother and had a conversation and said, "It's time for the kids to get some religion." And my grandmother said, "I don't care what faith they are, as long as they're not heathens and that they believe in God." As long as we were in Abrahamic faiths, it wouldn't be a problem.

Because of the neighborhood I grew up in and the environment I grew up in, I had a lot of Black role models around me. The Bay Area, and San Francisco specifically, was an environment with a kind of watered-down Black identity. There was an effort to water down culture for the sake of "capitalism" and "progressive politics," and I'll put that in air quotes. But for me, I always wondered how to settle, align, and reconcile being Black and being Jewish, versus being multiples of anything. I would go to church with my grandmother's family and sit in church and think that God was sophisticated enough to figure out that I was Jewish inside of a church context. And if I prayed or if I sang a hymn or whatever, I wasn't worried that God would be confused about what I was doing. Why would I not be true to my family and singing a hymn? God has to be more intelligent than our human limitations in that way.

So I grew up in this environment called St. Francis Square in San Francisco, California. It was founded by the Black longshoremen in 1969. There were white folks, but they were mostly in Hunters Point. And I was in the Western Addition, which is where the city put all the Black people and all the Japanese who had come out of internment camps. There was nothing but housing projects, from Laguna Street, which is the street I lived on, all the way up Turk Street to Divisadero Street, which is blocks and blocks. I grew up looking at a project called the Pink Palace outside my bedroom window. Every year, the kids from the Pink Palace would come over and steal my bike and kick my ass. I would go over there with a radical white Jewish mom—not my own, but a neighbor mom—and we would have twenty dollars and say, "Can we get my bike back?"

In the housing co-op, it was Black folks in leadership. Because it was a co-op, you had to have an annual meeting to change things. You had to have a quorum, so I went and studied and watched as it all happened. We had solar panels in 1975, and across the street, across Geary Boulevard, was all Japanese. Mrs. Richardson was two buildings over, and she would stand out on her porch and watch me like a hawk. My mom would say,

"Oh, you did this or that," and I would say, "How did you know?" She'd say, "Mrs. Richardson told me." I grew up with Rebecca, her daughter, in the same housing complex. Timmy Olsen lived on the other side of the square. And my neighborhood was full of Jewish communists, and the first non-lawyer for the San Francisco Lawyers Guild lived in the same building. She was all about freeing the brothers from Attica, a "correctional facility" in New York State. So it was just kind of a radical, sunny community with lots of Black folks.

I never swayed from Judaism, but I never felt like I had to pick one over the other. I mostly felt like I had to grow and really understand myself as a Black woman, particularly being raised by a white mom. My year between undergrad and graduate school in Washington, DC was a chance to deep-dive into what it was like to be Black, because I was coming from San Francisco, where it was kind of okay to be biracial. There were no biracial students in DC in my circle, so I spent an entire year just being totally myself but in an entirely different Black context. There were shades of Black, and there were people from all kinds of countries in Africa and the Caribbean, and all of that was really great for me. Then I came back to San Francisco, and in graduate school I ended up at Mills College, where I became part of the Black women's collective. Growing up in the Western Addition and that post-sixties, early-seventies Black culture heavily influenced my early identity.

When I think about the hope, courage, and heart needed to show up as your real, authentic self, I think that any time I had a major failure in my life, it was because my life was out of alignment. I was disconnected from myself. I would say that in my professional space and in my personal life, just growing into myself, I have had what I would like to call failures that I've had to re-narrate in some way and reframe in order to re-understand as successes. There were situations where it was between life and death, and I had to make a choice, and maybe that choice was an expression of bravery or an expression of courage. But I would say in some ways it came from not necessarily a desperate place, but a place where it was very clear that I had no other choice.

I'm thinking about myself now as a leader in this organization, and I think I would characterize myself as much more comfortable with myself. I can really show up as my authentic self, whatever that means. When I teach or when I present, I might change my cadence, I might change whatever, but I'm gonna try to be real the whole time.

The biggest, scariest moments have been when I've either taken a leap of faith or had to ask for help. I spent so much of my early career either being an imposter or having imposter syndrome. Everything from how I dressed to how I conducted myself was really in response to or anticipating the white gaze and then figuring out how to calibrate myself against that. I've had to really watch my sisters ahead of me who I read as confident, whole, and grounded. When they enter their space, I can see the roots under their feet, and in some ways, I've had to take that as giving myself permission: "Oh, if so-and-so can do that, I can do that too." I can get away with being myself and being in my body and being in my spirit and being in my excellence in that way. I have had to work on owning my excellence, where it lives inside of me, and being able to talk about it without feeling like it's an expression of hubris.

To feel grounded in my body, which supports bravery, I do superhero poses before I have to do something. You will find me in my bathroom, or my green room, or wherever I am, going through a whole process. I meditate every day, I walk or run pretty much every day, three or four miles in the morning, and I'm very, very aware that I have a lot of glitter flowing through me. I'm always a tiny bit agitated, so I have a lot of consciousness around that. I really worked to settle it, because when it's settled, that's where my system finds its physics. It's not in the agitation, and it's not even responding to the agitation. It's about having the capacity to settle my own agitation around it. When people are passionate and when people are in their power, there can really be a lot of energy in that space. My challenge in my invitation is to channel some of that energy into my feet.

The fact that each one of us is here doing whatever it is that's important to us, if we choose to just live that, then it means our work is not done because we're working. Then the question becomes "For what purpose? And what way?" and in the biggest picture, "What's the opportunity?"

Courage and hope give us new openings. They create new opportunities. Courage, bravery, and heart require us to engage in multiple levels and multiple ways, which is exactly how we're designed to engage. Courage, bravery, and heart encourage us to be whole. We need to engage these parts of ourselves that sometimes don't get invited in. It's about finding our true capacity—about being integrated and whole. Whatever happens, the physics creates something new and mysterious and beautiful.

MINDFULNESS PRACTICE: MINDFUL WALKING
Time Required: 5 minutes minimum

The capacity to walk is a great gift of life, and I don't take it for granted. Both of my brothers are disabled and lack the ability to walk with ease. As was stated in the introduction, meditation is not one-size-fits-all. To practice mindful walking, consider your needs, support, access, and circumstances and adapt the practice accordingly. An alternate practice when using a wheelchair may be to bring kind attention to the ground beneath you and to the sound of the wheels touching the ground.

One of the most beautiful ways that I know to come home to myself is through walking. Often when I am wrestling with choices and challenges, with a sense of purpose, direction, and meaning, I go outside on a long walk. I put the worries and choices aside to allow them air to breath, to rediscover the wisdom that is already here that I cannot see or feel. I am reminded of the Latin phrase *Solvitur ambulando*, "it is solved by walking." Walking seems to "solve" whatever might be holding me captive in the moment. Walking is a way to cultivate wisdom grounded in the body and alive to the environment in the moment.

One of the most delightful and transformational mindfulness practices I learned from Thich Nhat Hanh and the Plum Village community is mindful walking. With this practice, you walk with ease and freedom from worries and strife. As you walk, you allow yourself to focus on your steps, your breath, the environment—not to bypass difficulties but to nourish yourself and recognize the true gift it is to be alive. (However, this practice can be done anywhere—for example, walking from your car to the office or from one room to another.)

- Stand comfortably with eyes open.

- Choose an uncluttered, peaceful place to practice walking mindfully.

- Stand and feel the ground.

- As you prepare to walk, notice the shift of weight from one foot to the next.

- Feel your steps and your in- and out-breath.

- Shift your focus from "getting somewhere" (future focused) to "being here now" (present focused).

- Continue walking with mindful awareness, noticing your breath, body, and environment.

- When you are ready, pause and notice how you feel.

QUERIES

The following queries are from the Bethesda Friends Meeting website. Please visit their website for further details.[9]

Queries for Individuals from Bethesda Friends Meeting, Bethesda, Maryland

- How do the ways in which I choose to use my time, my possessions, my money, and my energy reflect my most deeply held values?

- To what extent is my sense of justice based in love?

- How do I seek truth by which to live? How do I know it when I find it? In what ways does my life speak of my beliefs and values? In what way is my life out of harmony with the truth as I know it? Why?

Queries for Groups from Bethesda Friends Meeting

- What efforts are we making as a community to become better acquainted with the sources of our spiritual heritage and the contributions of other religions and philosophies?

- How do we as individuals and as a community support one another in nurturing those gifts and in our search for a simpler life?

- As we work for peace in the world, how are we nourished by peace within and among ourselves?

AFTERWORD

I'm incredibly grateful that we've taken this journey together and are finding not an ending but rather a beginning. This book, my journey and yours, is a pilgrimage. And as pilgrims do, we continue on, even after we've walked the last miles or read the last page.

Before the pandemic changed everything, I led many pilgrimages on El Camino de Santiago, Spain; the last one was in 2019. I led two separate groups of pilgrims along the coastal trails, the hills, and villages, through downpours, high wind, and bright sunshine to Finisterre, a place known since ancient times as the End of Land, the westernmost point on the pilgrimage of El Camino. Little more than a windswept rock, this profoundly sacred place—often referred to as a "thin" place because the separation between the sacred and the material worlds is thin—is often overtaken by tour buses and hawkers at souvenir shops selling trinkets and tiny replicas of the lighthouse of Finisterre.

The day our group arrived, having walked a few hundred kilometers and now the final kilometer uphill to the lighthouse, we were buoyed along by grace more than gravity. When we arrived, I left the group behind and walked out past the shops, past the crowds, past the tourists taking selfies, to a rock perched out over the Atlantic Ocean. It felt like I was there for hours. Time stood still. All I could see was water, water everywhere, low-lying clouds, and more water. I sat there, staring out. It all became so clear: *I am complete. This is complete. I've done what I set out to do. Yes, there were ups and downs. Yes, it was hard. Yes, it was beautiful. And I am complete.* I looked again at the water and then turned to go.

ACKNOWLEDGMENTS

In 2019 I began writing this book just before the global pandemic. Today as we emerge into a post-pandemic world, I am holding the spirit of rededication, reemergence, and hope for a truly transformed society, radically different as we individually and collectively navigate how to live in a world where hope leans forward. I began writing this book in New Hope, Pennsylvania, the traditional territory of the Lenni Lenape Nation, and I end this book on the ancestral lands of the Tewa, currently known as Santa Fe, New Mexico. I am grateful to these land stewards for their wisdom, guidance, culture, and legacy.

Writing a book, like other acts of love and hope, is not undertaken alone. It takes a community, and I am grateful to many people. Thank you to my family members who have always been a source of love and inspiration, and in particular: Lewis Brown; Katie Lynne Brown; Sophia Pinto; Milton Pinto, III; Jason Holtham; Maya Holtham; Daliah Farrar; David Mansfield; and Maggie Greenwald. To my "adopted" family, and especially Chris Grygo and Marcia Lee, boundless thanks. Thank you to my dear friends Kirsten Olson and Karen Erlichman, who were early readers of the manuscript and offered invaluable insight. Thank you to Joan Broadfield, who supported me through early edits and spent many hours reading the book aloud with me, as well as offering guidance on Quaker faith and practice. I am grateful to my friend Kaira Jewel Lingo, who offered important resources at a crucial time. Thank you to Brenda Harrington, my Georgetown "journal partner" of many years, who cheered me on. Yet again, I realize the importance of having people who support me in maintaining wellness in body, mind, and spirit, and for that I am grateful to Mahan Rishi and Nirbhe Kaur Singh Khalsa, Ilona Melker, Chris Strickland, and Dr. Jennifer Luan. I am grateful to spiritual friends and mentors who supported and encouraged me, including Lyn Fine, John Bell, and Viviane Ephraimson-Abt, as well as Sister Peace, Marisela Gomez, and the ARISE (Awakening through Race, Instersectionality, and Social Equity) Sangha.

I have endless gratitude to Lil Copan of Broadleaf Books for countless hours reading, massaging, editing, and generally being there for me with extraordinary patience and kindness, as well as the entire team at Broadleaf, including Erin Gibbons, Elle Rogers, and Karen Schenkenfelder. I am incredibly grateful to Natascha Bruckner, an amazing editor who helped me think through the material on mindfulness in the Plum Village community. I want to offer a big thank you to Ebonie Ledbetter for support with skillful structural editing. I am holding deep gratitude to all those who read the first draft of the book and offered an early endorsement. Your support meant everything.

This book could not be completed without the love, kindness, and support of the Upaya Zen Center in Santa Fe, New Mexico, specifically Roshi Joan Halifax and the community that cooked, cleaned, chanted, and supported me at a crucial time when I was dangerously exhausted from an onslaught of life's complications.

To all profiled in "Real Voices, Real Courage"—eli tizcareño, LoAn Nguyen, George Lakey, Susan Cross, Brian Braganza, Francisco Burgos, Fanny Brewster, and Ilana Kaufman: thank you for sharing your life, hope, and courage.

NOTES

Introduction

1. For a deeper understanding of the term *spiritual direction*, please refer to "What Is Spiritual Direction and Companionship?," Spiritual Directors International, https://tinyurl.com/4e5ypr8u.

2. Joanna Macy and Chris Johnstone, *Active Hope: How to Face the Mess We're in without Going Crazy* (Novato, CA: New World Library, 2012).

3. Joan Halifax, "Wise Hope in Social Engagement," UPAYA Institute and Zen Center, July 2, 2019. https://www.upaya.org/2019/07/wise-hope-in-social-engagement-by-roshi-joan-halifax/.

4. St. Teresa of Avila, *St. Teresa of Jesus of the Order of Our Lady of Carmel: Embracing the Life, Relations, Maxims and Foundations* (Columbus Press, 1911), 75.

5. Pema Chodron, *Comfortable with Uncertainty* (Boston: Shambhala, 2003).

6. Patricia Loring, *Spiritual Discernment: the context and goal of clearness committees.* Pendle Hill Pamphlet #305 (Wallingford, PA, 1992), 9.

7. Rebecca Solnit, "We Could Be Heroes: An Election-Year Letter," *Guardian*, October 15, 2021, https://tinyurl.com/3vnmnfuk.

8. Gabrielle Roth. *Maps to Ecstasy: The Healing Power of Movement* (New World Library, 1998). Pages xv–xvi.

9. Gregory Kramer. "Insight Dialogue: Interpersonal Mindfulness and Compassion." https://gregorykramer.org.

10. While the actual date of the principle is unknown, it is associated with the writing of the Great Law of Haudenosaunee Confederacy, 1142–1500 CE. See "Culture and History: Values," Haudenosaunee Confederacy, https://www.haudenosauneeconfederacy.com/values/.

11. "The Varieties of Contemplative Experience," Brown University, Clinical and Affective Neuroscience Laboratory, https://tinyurl.com/2s4a349s.

Chapter 1

1. Epigraph: Elizabeth Lesser, *Broken Open: How Difficult Times Can Help Us Grow* (New York: Villard, 2005).
2. Parker J. Palmer, "Chapter 1: The Primacy of Soul," Center for Courage & Renewal, published on YouTube, December 9, 2015, https://tinyurl.com/2apmbekw.
3. Gregory Orr, *How Beautiful the Beloved* (Port Townsend, WA: Copper Canyon, 2009), 55. Used with permission.
4. Margaret J. Wheatley, "The Place beyond Fear and Hope," *Shambhala Sun*, March 2009, 79–83, available at https://margaretwheatley.com/library/articles/.
5. Mark Nepo, *Unlearning Back to God: Essays on Inwardness, 1985–2005* (New York: Khaniqahi Nimatullahi, 2006), reprinted at https://marknepo.com/books_unlearning.php.
6. Patricia Loring, *Spiritual Discernment: The Context and Goal of Clearness Committees*, Pendle Hill Pamphlet no. 305 (Wallingford, PA: Pendle Hill, 1992).
7. Clarissa Pinkola Estés, *Women Who Run with the Wolves: Myths and Stories of the Wild Woman Archetype* (New York: Ballantine, 1996).
8. For the "Real Voices, Real Courage" stories, profiled subjects' words have been lightly edited for clarity.

Chapter 2

1. John O'Donohue, *Anam Cara: A Book of Celtic Wisdom* (New York: Cliff Street, 1997).
2. O'Donohue, *Anam Cara*.
3. James Hollis, *Living an Examined Life: Wisdom for the Second Half of the Journey* (Boulder, CO: Sounds True, 2018).

4. Bill Plotkin, *The Journey of Soul Initiation: A Field Guide for Visionaries, Evolutionaries, and Revolutionaries* (Novato, CA: New World Library, 2021).

5. https://insightdialogue.org.

Chapter 3

1. "What Is the Eightfold Path?," Lion's Roar, July 21, 2016, https://www.lionsroar.com/what-is-eightfold-path/. Used with permission.

2. Parker J. Palmer, "The Politics of the Brokenhearted: On Holding the Tensions of Democracy," in *Deepening the American Dream: Reflections on the Inner Life and Spirit of Democracy* (San Francisco: Jossey-Bass, 2005), available at the Center for Courage & Renewal website, https://couragerenewal.org.

3. Brené Brown, *Daring Greatly: How the Courage to Be Vulnerable Transforms the Way We Live, Love, Parent, and Lead* (New York: Avery, 2012).

Chapter 4

1. Parker J. Palmer, *Let Your Life Speak: Listening for the Voice of Vocation* (San Francisco: Jossey-Bass, 2000).

2. James Hollis, *Swamplands of the Soul: New Life in Dismal Places* (Toronto: Inner City, 1996).

3. Louise Erdrich, *The Painted Drum* (New York: Harper, 2019).

4. Emily Dickinson, "'Hope' Is the Thing with Feathers (314)," in *The Complete Poems of Emily Dickinson*, edited by Thomas H. Johnson (Cambridge, MA: Belknap, 1983), available on the Poetry Foundation website, https://www.poetryfoundation.org.

5. "Anthem," Leonard Cohen, Spotify, track 5 on *The Future*, Sony Music Entertainment, 1992.

6. Thich Nhat Hanh, *How to Love* (Berkeley: Parallax, 2015).

7. Rick Hanson, PhD. "Take in the Good." https://www.rickhanson.net/take-in-the-good/.

8. John O'Donohue, *Eternal Echoes: Celtic Reflections on Our Yearning to Belong* (New York: HarperCollins Publishers, 2000), p. 156.

Chapter 5

1. Epigraph: Jill Satterfield, "Meditation in Motion," January 23, 2014, https://jillsatterfield.org, originally published in *Tricycle* magazine.
2. Valerie Brown, *The Road That Teaches: Lessons in Transformation through Travel* (Philadelphia: QuakerPress, 2012).
3. Donna Farhi, *The Breathing Book: Good Health and Vitality through Essential Breath Work* (New York: Owl, 1996).

Chapter 6

1. Bianca DiJulio, Liz Hamel, Cailey Muñana, and Mollyann Brodie, *Loneliness and Social Isolation in the United States, the United Kingdom, and Japan: An International Survey*, Kaiser Family Foundation, August 30, 2018, https://tinyurl.com/2p8655yu.
2. National Academies of Sciences, Engineering, and Medicine. 2020. *Social Isolation and Loneliness in Older Adults: Opportunities for the Health Care System*. Washington, DC: The National Academies Press. https://doi.org/10.17226/25663.
3. Julianne Holt-Lunstad, Timothy B. Smith, Mark Baker, Tyler Harris, and David Stephenson, "Loneliness and Social Isolation as Risk Factors for Mortality: A Meta-analytic Review," *Perspectives of Psychological Science*, March 11, 2015, https://doi.org/10.1177%2F1745691614568352.
4. Parker J. Palmer, *A Place Called Community*, Pendle Hill Pamphlet no. 212 (Wallingford, PA: Pendle Hill, 1977).
5. David Budbill, "This Morning," in *Poetry of Presence: An Anthology of Mindfulness Poems*, ed. Phyllis Cole-Dai and Ruby R. Wilson (West Hartford, CT: Grayson, 2017).
6. To learn more about the practice of beginning anew, see Sister Chan Khong, *Beginning Anew: Four Steps to Restoring Communication* (Berkeley: Parallax, 2014).
7. You may wish to visit the Plum Village website or read Sister Chan Khong's book *Beginning Anew* to learn about the practice in greater detail.

Chapter 7

1. Richard Strozzi-Heckler, *The Leadership Dojo: Building Your Foundation as an Exemplary Leader* (Berkeley, CA: Frog Books, 2007).

2. Galway Kinnell, "Saint Francis and the Sow," in *Three Books* (Boston: Houghton Mifflin, 2002).

3. For more on the topic of clearness committees, see Valerie Brown, *Coming to Light: Deepening Connectedness, Clarity, and Community through the Clearness Committee*, Pendle Hill Pamphlet no. 446 (Wallingford, PA: Pendle Hill, 2017).

Chapter 8

1. Epigraph: Linda Hogan, *The Woman Who Watches Over the World: A Native Memoir* (New York: Norton, 2001).

2. Daniel Goleman, *Focus: The Hidden Driver of Excellence* (New York: Harper, 2013).

3. Ronald Heifetz, Alexander Grashow, and Marty Linsky, *The Practice of Adaptive Leadership: Tools and Tactics for Changing Your Organization and the World* (Boston: Harvard Business Press, 2009).

4. Kelli Harding, *The Rabbit Effect: Live Longer, Happier, and Healthier with the Groundbreaking Science of Kindness* (New York: Atria, 2019).

5. Anthony Burrow, "What is Purpose?" YouTube video, 4:04, January 14, 2013. https://www.youtube.com/watch?v=2Lljvmt572M.

6. Jan Richardson, "The Inside Door." Quoted on *Mystic Meandering*. April 19, 2019. https://mysticmeandering.blogspot.com/2019/04/the-inside-door-jan-richardson.html.

7. James Hollis, *What Matters Most: Living a More Considered Life* (New York: Gotham, 2009).

8. James Hollis, *Living an Examined Life: Wisdom for the Second Half of the Journey* (Boulder, CO: Sounds True, 2018).

9. "Queries," Bethesda Friends Meeting, Bethesda, MD, https://www.bethesdafriends.org/Monthly-Queries.

ABOUT THE AUTHOR

Valerie Brown, JD, MA, PCC

Valerie Brown is an author, Buddhist-Quaker Dharma teacher, facilitator, and executive coach specializing in leadership development and mindfulness practices with a focus on diversity, social equity, and inclusion. A former lawyer and lobbyist, Valerie transformed her high-pressure, twenty-year career into serving leaders and nonprofits to create trustworthy, authentic, compassionate, and connected workspaces.

An award-winning author, her books include *The Road that Teaches: Lessons in Transformation through Travel, The*

Mindful School Leader: Practices to Transform Your Leadership and School (with Kirsten Olson, PhD), and *Cultivating Happiness, Resilience, and Well-Being through Meditation, Mindfulness, and Movement: A Guide for Educators* (contributor).

She is an ordained Buddhist Dharma teacher in the lineage of Zen Master Thich Nhat Hanh and the Plum Village tradition and facilitates national and international gatherings and retreats for nonprofits and corporations and leads an annual pilgrimage to El Camino de Santiago, Spain to celebrate the power of sacred places. She is a certified Kundalini yoga teacher (500 hours), engaging leaders to embody somatic wisdom and creativity.

An accredited leadership coach, she is the Founder and Chief Mindfulness Officer of Lead Smart Coaching, LLC, supporting leaders to apply and integrate leadership and mindfulness for greater resilience, clarity, and compassion, and is a co-director of Georgetown's Institute for Transformational Leadership.

Valerie's unique and extensive training blends social justice, evidenced-based mindfulness practices, leadership development, and spiritual growth. She holds a Juris Doctor from Howard University School of Law, Master of Arts from Miami University (Ohio), and Bachelor of Arts from City University of New York.

Of Afro-Cuban descent, Valerie is a member of the Religious Society of Friends (Quakers) and lives and tends a lively perennial home garden in New Hope, PA.

www.valeriebrown.us